OMG!
YOUR BEST MIND EVER

How to Make Your Brain Work for You, Change Your Mind and Habits and Live The Life of Your Dream

Steve Meyer

© **Copyright 2021 by Steve Meyer - All rights reserved.**

The content contained within this book may not be reproduced, duplicated or transmitted without direct written permission from the author or the publisher.

Under no circumstances will any blame or legal responsibility be held against the publisher, or author, for any damages, reparation, or monetary loss due to the information contained within this book. Either directly or indirectly.

Legal Notice:

This book is copyright protected. This book is only for personal use. You cannot amend, distribute, sell, use, quote or paraphrase any part, or the content within this book, without the consent of the author or publisher.

Disclaimer Notice:

Please note the information contained within this document is for educational and entertainment purposes only. All effort has been executed to present accurate, up to date, and reliable, complete information. No warranties of any kind are declared or implied. Readers acknowledge that the author is not engaging in the rendering of legal, financial, medical or professional advice. The content within this book has been derived from various sources. Please consult a licensed professional before attempting any techniques outlined in this book.

By reading this document, the reader agrees that under no circumstances is the author responsible for any losses, direct or indirect, which are incurred as a result of the use of information contained within this document, including, but not limited to, — errors, omissions, or inaccuracies.

Download Your Free Gift

Before you go any further, why not pick up a gift from us to you?

GROWTH PRINCIPLES

If you're willing to learn and transform yourself in all the right areas,

then success is definitely for you.

So, to find out how you can do that, let's get reading.

Scan the barcode to get it before it expires!

Table Of Contents

Introduction..7

Chapter 1: How Your Mind Interacts with Your Environment and How Your Brain is Driving Your Life..................................11

Chapter 2: Understanding Stress.......................................16

Chapter 3: Where Is Your Stress Coming From?......................25

Chapter 4: Impact of Stress on Health................................29

Chapter 5: When Stress Becomes Chronic.............................34

    Signs of Chronic Stress..35

Chapter 6: What You Think, Matters..................................43

Chapter 7: A Step-By-Step Guide to Tackling Stress Head-On......63

Chapter 8: Managing a Stressed Brain.................................74

    Identifying Source of Stress...76

    Being Aware of Stress Signs..79

    Finding Response for a Quick Stress Relief......................80

    Making Time for Fun and Relaxation.............................88

    Learning to Connect with Others..................................89

    Making Quick Stress Relief a Habit...............................90

    Managing Your Time Better..91

Making Exercise a Habit...*92*

Changing Your Lifestyle..*94*

Chapter 9: How to Overcome and Reduce Stress and Anxiety?......96

Chapter 10: Destress Your Mind and Soul..101

Control Your Thoughts...*101*

Manage Your Emotions..*109*

Chapter 11: Social, Spiritual, and Environmental, Strategies for Stress Relief..118

Sensory Immersion..*118*

Reducing Stress with Tai Chi, Yoga, and Pilates..........................*121*

Stress Inoculation Therapy..*124*

Chapter 12: Leave Stress Behind. Live A Happier Life...................127

Conclusion..130

Thank You!...134

Download Your Free Gift..135

Introduction

Do you want to learn how to make your brain work for you, change your mind and habits, and live the life of your dreams?

Have you ever wanted something but couldn't do it? Have you wanted something so badly that it kept taking over your thoughts? Have you ever tried really hard to get something only for it not happen in the end and then felt like a failure even though all you did was try? Do not feel defeated because when this happens there are steps that can be taken to help alleviate some of these negative feelings.

Have you ever been so stressed out that you didn't know what to do with yourself?

Do you want to learn how to relax and manage stressful situations?

Have you ever thought your life was over or that the worst was going to happen or just wanted the stress to stop?

Are you Dealing with anxiety, depression, PTSD, or trauma related issues?

This is actually going on in your conscious and subconscious mind. The subconscious mind is the part of your mind where all of your habits are stored. That is why you tend to react the same way each time something stressful happens in your life. The first thing people say when they want to change their lives is "I need to change my thinking. I need to change my habits. I need to stop reacting that way."

How often do you get into a stressful situation and you go through the same pattern over and over again?

Have you ever wanted something so bad that it just seems like it will never happen?

Have you ever been so stressed out that even the smallest things trigger feelings of stress if not dealt with properly?

Do you want to learn how many times in your life have been impacted negatively because of stress or anxiety and how to change your thinking and habits related to those negative experiences?

If you answered yes to any or all of these questions, then this book is for you. When we are stressed or anxious our brain goes into fight-or-flight mode. This is due to the amygdala, which activates certain areas in the brain that control our responses. When this happens, your brain stops you from thinking rationally and you just react in the way your habits tell you to react. I used to be anxious all the time and I didn't know how to change that bad thinking.

I used to be so stressed about my job that I would go into panic attacks for no apparent reason.

I used to get triggered by things that used to not bother me before and just seemed like a hassle now.

I was tired of feeling like I was living my life in reverse.

Is there anything you can do? Yes, yes there is! Stress Management is one of the biggest things holding us back from achieving our goals, which means we need it at all times. Your life will be much easier if you can relax and eliminate anxiety and stress from your life at any cost. Once the stress is gone, you will see things so clearly and be able to achieve your goals by eliminating those bad habits that have been holding you back.

Once this happens you need to know how to make your brain work for you and how habits are formed. The wrong type of thinking can keep us from our goals as much as anything else.

How many times a day do you get stressed out? How many times a day do you find yourself reacting exactly the way a habit tells you to react? How often is stress holding back what would otherwise be an amazing life? The answer is more times than not.

I hope that this book helps you to be able to change the way your brain is wired and not react in the same way as it has told you to do before. Read this book and take notes. Decide what works for you and what doesn't. What makes you feel better, calmer, happier?

This is one of those books that everyone should read but unfortunately most people never get around to reading it because they think it is "too much work" or "too complicated." You will soon see that everyone can benefit from the techniques in this book. My goal is that once you finish reading this book, you can change your habits, your thinking and become happier, healthier and manage your stress more easily than ever before.

Chapter 1: How Your Mind Interacts with Your Environment and How Your Brain is Driving Your Life

Most people don't understand how the brain works. They mistakenly believe that their mental habits are fixed. But your brain is constantly changing, and this makes it possible to change the way you think, feel, and behave. When your mind is interacting with your environment in a way that helps you meet your needs for pleasure or avoidance of pain, it increases the likelihood of recreating those experiences in the future. This creates what has been called a "habit loop."

A habit loop consists of a cue, a routine, and a reward. The cue can be an event, such as walking by a bakery. The routine is the way your mind reacts. You think about how good it would taste to eat a donut or cake. You feel your mouth begin to water because your salivary glands are being activated. Your digestive system releases digestive juices and the muscles of your mouth and tongue are working in anticipation in saliva glands of taste buds working to stimulate pleasure centers in the brain when you actually do eat it.

You might also be planning to buy it for later or fantasizing about how good the cake would taste. You might be celebrating a special occasion, such as your birthday, or visiting with friends.

your reward is a combination of changes in your body chemistry (chemical changes in the brain) that reduces your stress, makes you feel good (such as serotonin), and creates positive thoughts that are familiar and pleasurable. If you delay eating the cake until another time and then eat it while thinking about having come back to get it, this can become part of the loop too. Since you are actively involved in setting up these loops in your mind, you should be able to manipulate them to create any outcome you want.

A cue is anything that triggers your mind to begin a loop. This could be something you hear, read, or see. Once you have identified your cues, you can use them to activate your loop. For example, if you walk by a bakery and smell the donuts in the window and feel an intense craving for them or want to go in, this could be a cue to start your habit loop. You might then think about how delicious they would taste and begin planning your visit or response to this cue. When you try to talk yourself out of going into the bakery while feeling the craving, it turns out that it is more difficult than just doing what really needs to be done. You'd probably go into the bakery and buy the donuts.

The habits we form determine how we think, feel, and behave daily. They create our personality, who you are as a person. Our reactions to life's events are already stored in our minds and ready for use when triggered by cues. We're not just reacting to what is happening in the moment; we're reacting according to how we've learned to react from past experience. In order to change the way that you react, then it is necessary to change your habits of thinking and behaving.

The brain is capable of creating many different types of thoughts, feelings, and beliefs. It is also capable of creating new connections between the neurons in its network. Connections are made with neurotransmitters, which are chemicals that carry messages through our synapses. Your brain can use the same or different neurotransmitters to create new thoughts and feelings. If the circuits you want to activate are not getting the messages they need, there is something wrong with your cue-routine-reward system that needs correction. The cause could be an environmental factor or a cognitive factor such as a way you're thinking about your problem; something from your past experience; some kind of negative thinking pattern, or a belief that is causing you stress or fear.

There are many different ways to modify your habits and change your brain. You can do it by yourself, by working with others, or by being in the presence of a therapist or professional. You can experiment to find out what works for you. When you carefully consider what is happening in your mind at any given moment, you will be able to determine which cues can be used to help create the results you want. As more things are happening around you, including all of their associated cues and rewards, it will be possible for your mind to react in a way that is consistent with what it has learned from experience. This is how your mind can become an ally, not a prisoner.

Habits re-wire the pathways of your brain and if you want to change these habits, the only way to do it is through the formation of new habits. The most efficient method for doing this is through repetition and reinforcement of new behaviors until they become automatic. As soon as you experience any kind of stress or react in a way that feels familiar, but you'd rather not be experiencing it again, its time to take charge of your mind. The first step that's important is being alert to what is happening in your mind by anticipating how you'll react next. You can then learn to recognize the cues and start your cue-routine-reward loop in such a way that is entirely different from how you've been conditioned to react. This is why it's so important to take control of your mind and learn how to change your habits and behaviors.

Our habits determine our lifestyle. Once there are new habits that have taken hold, we're not actively choosing them anymore. We are being guided by these new ways of thinking, feeling, and behaving that have become automatic like breathing. Our automatic behaviors become second nature; we become habituated to them, until they come naturally as we go about our day without even thinking about them. When we are habituated, our behavior is less flexible, and we become more predictable.

When you're habituated to certain behaviors, you will do them without thinking about them, just like breathing; or the fact that you're having a conversation with someone. When you're habituated to your habits, it is likely that your motivation for doing something changes as well. Habits can be bad or good depending on the type of habits they are and the values that are involved in implementing them. For example, when a habit is harmful or destructive to yourself or others in some way such as smoking cigarettes, drinking alcohol, overeating food or being addicted to drugs, there's a solution: stop doing it. When it comes to more beneficial habits, such as exercising regularly (fitness), good eating habits (slimming), practicing yoga or meditation, being kind to others (good neighbor), doing the tasks that you need to do so that you can maintain your job or business or be productive in life (productive), or being a good parent and creating a harmonious family environment, there's probably no need for any kind of self-help method to change them.

Every habit that we have in life is usually the result of a learned process. The first step to creating or re-creating a new habit is to make a conscious choice about what it is you want to do and how you want to feel and behave. Your decision will be based on how you want your life and family to look like, what kind of person you would like to be, and how you wish others would treat you. You should take these criteria into account as you decide about what changes need to be made in your life in order for things to become better.

Chapter 2: Understanding Stress

The doctor leaned forward in his chair towards Paul and said, "You need to stop right now, accept help, or there's every possibility that you're going to die."

Paul was icy numb to what he was being told. He had been living, or rather existing the same way for months and the whirlpool of life had now sucked him so far down that he didn't know how to emerge back to the surface. Any feelings that he once had were encased in a glacier-thick layer that wasn't about to melt anytime soon.

Paul was a CEO of a tech company, and his customers appreciated his products and services so much that as the value and quantity of contracts increased, his company grew in the space of three years from 20 employees to over eighty. Paul became a frequent flyer, traveling weekly throughout North America meeting with new and existing customers. Clinging to the style of work that he'd implemented when starting his company, he believed that managing each employee and client and project was his responsibility. The delegation wasn't an option, and like NASA's Apollo 13 moon landing mission he believed that the phrase "Failure Is Not an Option" applied to him too. He'd built the company singlehanded by networking and personally following through with clients, providing the best products and personal service that he would have expected for himself. Requests to meet with a new or existing client were usually scheduled to meet with him in person, not a colleague. He'd often arrive home after one o'clock in the morning and would be back at his desk a little over four hours later. He told himself that he was providing for his family, yet he rarely saw them, and even on special occasions like his child's birthday, he'd only be home long enough to celebrate and see his child settled in bed before he was working away at his computer.

That was his routine until March 2019 when he collapsed with crushing chest pain onto the cold floor tiles in his bathroom. He was forty-one years old.

The extreme unending struggle to be everything to everyone created the perfect storm where Paul suddenly succumbed to heart disease that was brought on by months and months of extreme stress and eventual burnout. And Paul is not alone. We'll follow up on what happened to him later in the book.

At the present moment, too many people are bombarded from all sides to the extent that we're in a constant state of alarm and the statistics show that we're slowly sinking into a stinky quagmire thanks to stress.

In 2018, a British survey of over 4600 men and women found that three out of every four persons were stressed to the point of feeling overwhelmed or unable to manage, with one-third of those feeling suicidal, with women feeling more pressured and suicidal than males. In the United States, the situation is even worse, with stress affecting four out of every five employees; that's about a whopping 104 million employees out of 130 million full-time employees. Looking to the future, young adults are also impacted with studies showing an unacceptably high increase in reports of anxiety and depression, which if not addressed has the potential to become a significant health problem as they enter the workforce.

The Top Seven Causes of Stress

These are a vicious circle, both feeding the cause and feeding off the effects of the cause. Here they are in descending order:

1. *Sleep*

The lack of, or poor-quality sleep is a culprit. The less sleep that you have, the more symptoms you have, including early waking, fatigue, and less productivity. It also creates an inability to release adrenaline and other hormones.

2. *Media Overload*

Some people physically exhaust themselves with media overload, binging on television, and spending too much time in social media. This affects their ability to make good and solid decisions.

3. *Poor Nutrition*

Caffeine, processed foods, and refined sugar all contribute to inadequate nutrition. As stress levels rise, many people do not eat properly, which in turn creates another vicious cycle.

4. *Relationships*

Another major source of stress is divorce, the death of a spouse or close relative, and disagreements with friends. In addition, isolation and loneliness are added stressors within our lives.

5. Health

Health is another area that can be further compounded by the initial stress that is created by a catastrophic illness or an accident that can further compound stress, impacting our lives and relationships.

6. Money

Personal finance is a main stressor. Beyond the regular cost-of-living stressors, there are expenses such as college loans, children's education, medical expenses, or a senior relative's care that all contribute to financial stress. Another enormous financial stressor is losing a job. The stress of repaying loans or being able to pay employees' wages can put a strain on one's relationships and health if you own or manage a business.

7. Job Pressure

You suspected that the workplace would be number one and you're right! What's causing the rise in stress? Long working hours, increased workloads, shorter deadlines, and increased expectation have all contributed to the rise in workplace anxiety and pressure, according to research from the past 20 years. Micromanaging or demeaning managers, the working environment, the job not living up to promises in the job description and interviews, long working hours, increased workloads, shorter deadlines, and increased expectation have all contributed to the rise in workplace anxiety and pressure. Co-worker tension also ranked second on the stress list, behind the number one stressor of workload. Combined, they account for 74% of reported workplace stress. One study showed that most people felt their co-workers were negative and needed help because they personally had felt the urge to strike out at co-workers!

Employers don't like to admit that what's happening at their company is an issue, yet research consistently shows that the workplace is the number one stressor. It's a deluge of pain, sucking in pressures and demands from all directions until the job becomes too much.

As employers, and employees, we need to do better at recognizing and reducing stressors and helping ourselves and our co-workers pinpoint what's important in order to create a balanced environment between a personal and professional life.

What type of stress is the issue?

You might think that it's the major stressors such as a divorce, death of a loved one, major surgery, moving to a new house, or a combination of any of them that is the main factor that's doing the most damage. However, a study led by Kate Leger from the university of California concluded that it's the little stressors that can have a seriously detrimental effect on the body too, negatively impacting the heart in particular. The researchers found that what would be considered a minor issue, such as unexpectedly being asked to work a deadline or having a minor argument with a friend could actually create a powerful negative effect, particularly if we keep a firm grip on what was causing us to be upset and continue to fret about it throughout the day.

A major stressor is a problem to be rid of. A small stress is not a trivial experience either.

If left unchecked, stress can become chronic which can lead to burnout, affecting the most hardworking employees and rendering them unable to function effectively on a personal or professional level. However, burnout doesn't happen suddenly. Its nature is insidious, slowly increasing over time like a slow leak. This stealthy approach of burnout makes it much harder to recognize compared to an immediate stressor. Still, the body and mind provide warnings during the burnout build-up.

In the following chapters I'll examine what's causing the rise in anxiety and pressure, its impact on the body, and outline different methods that you can use to identify the signs of stress in yourself. To reduce the physical and emotional impacts of stress and burnout, we'll look at how to spot triggers and test out several ways to determine which ones work best for you.

It's also necessary to have an assortment of methods or "tools" that you can draw on to address the varying and potentially stressful situations that you encounter. However, it's vital that you use the tools that you've learned and apply them. The tools become especially important when you detect that an event has the potential to be stressful or you suddenly find yourself plunged into a tense and demanding situation and must deal with the resulting stress as soon as you can. If you do nothing, even when you detect your body reacting to the stress, no amount of knowledge will help you without applying what you've learned.

Collectively and individually, we need to take stress and its detrimental impact seriously. We know what we should do, but not enough of us are taking preventive action. For example, when dealing with fire we have safety precautions in place and we actively protect ourselves, our property, and the environment from the dangers of fire and smoke as well as having trained professionals who can step in when a fire overwhelms, and a potential disaster ensues. We know the negative effects and we take fire seriously. If enough people started to pay attention to pressure and challenging circumstances in the workplace and noticing how it affected them, such as feeling their muscles tighten and noticing changes to the breath, and then applying stress-management tools to protect themselves from the harmful effects of stress then there would be fewer long-term damage to one's well-being and less impact to the workforce.

Likewise, if more employers took the impact of workplace stressors more seriously, then there would be increased productivity and less turnover. Policies and follow-through must be in place and managers trained to recognize potential stressors and be an example of a solution, not part of the problem.

This means that there's a lot at stake and while everyone's needs are different, this book will build upon what I've learned in my experience and from the latest research to demonstrate what can be done to achieve personal balance and go from stress to strength. Since 2005, I've been leading well-being programs, including mindfulness and stress-management techniques in group settings and online trainings. I've found that what works best is giving people different tools that they can personally choose to use; ones that suit their lifestyle or personality and their work schedule or professional environment.

We'll also examine stress and its impact on the body and mind, explore what can be done within a company to alleviate stress and mitigate complications, and outline a variety of methods that you as an individual can use to remove the barriers to a balanced life.

With over two decades teaching workplace well-being initiatives, I've learned that there's not a one-program-fits-all solution that is going to fix the problem of stress and prevent burnout. It may require several methods to first stabilize the problem area, replace one method with another as you slowly begin to free yourself from past habits and reactions, and finally reach a stage of stress recognition and prevention.

Stress is disruptive at best and destructive at its worst.

One recent stress-management program participant was Ellie. She dreaded going to her work in Boston as she no longer felt as capable as her colleagues. She was working full-time and attending college in the evening once a week. Balancing the daytime demands of work with evening deadlines for twenty-page reports that were to be handed in for her college class left her with no free time and her energy was draining away with no obvious means of replenishing. She was on the verge of dropping out of college due to insecurity in her once-confident talents and the stress of worrying if she would fail both her classwork and receive a terrible report from her employer. Fortunately, her manager sent Ellie and her team to complete the stress-management program where Ellie learned to initiate a self-care practice using some of the tangible techniques in this book and take back control of her life. By alleviating external pressures and self-doubt she eliminated the build-up of stress and burnout that was keeping her stuck in a position of real pain, and she not only graduated from college but was also promoted as a team leader at the start of the following year.

Every person needs to create his or her own individualized solution.

With both major and small stressors significantly posing an immediate and long-term health crisis we'll look at what worked for different people to help them crush the barriers to overcome their daily struggle with balancing stress in their working and private lives, and help you determine what can work for you too.

Chapter 3: Where Is Your Stress Coming From?

Hundreds of years ago we didn't live in metropolitan cities or towns and more likely lived-in villages, small hamlets, on ranches, or in a cabin in the forest. We had to fend for ourselves, or sometimes shared responsibilities with our neighbors. We had to fight for our land, hunt our foods and protect our families. We had nature to rely on for the procurement of our family.

As human beings, we have the fight-or-flight response, a physiological reaction that occurs when we perceive an attack. We go into this reaction automatically when we feel attacked, threatened, harassed, or otherwise at some risk of harm Walter Bradford Cannon theorized that animals react to threats with a general sympathetic discharge that primes the animal to either fight or flee for its life. The adrenal medulla produces hormonal secretions of catecholamine's, such as norepinephrine and epinephrine, which make the heartbeat faster, the senses go into hypersensitivity. This helps the animal survive in nature. Other names for the fight/flight, freeze/fawn, hyperarousal, or acute stress reaction in PTSD include fight/flight, freeze/fawn, hyperarousal, and acute stress response.

Our Ancestors Hunted

Our forefathers benefited from the fight or flight response. While our ancestors went out hunting for game as a group, they had to be aware of the animal's abilities and challenges. When the animal was found and ready for the kill, the hunters used their strategies to ensure that the hunt was as successful as possible. They had to be aware of the potential risks from the animal defending itself the same response of fight or flight. For the hunters the decision was based on a Fight for food or flight for safety if necessary.

It was a bold strategy of two men on the left flank, another two on the right flank, and a fifth who goes in for the kill. All hunters working together for a common goal, to kill the beast for food. Their bodies processed all the adrenaline and other hormones to their advantage, enhancing their agility and speed to better hold and maximize the use of weapons better hearing acuity helped them to listen to each other and other animals, their strong scents to their presence known.

As soon as the animal was killed the human body processed the used hormones and placed the body at rest. Once the animal had been butchered, taken to the village and distributed to the other families a big party ensued. The hunter's bodies cleansed the remaining hormones through eating, moving, and finally sleeping as the party went through the night. The next morning the hunters awoke refreshed and ready for the next hunting expedition. Stress free.

Our Ancestors Fought

The fight or flight response worked especially well when hunters were hunted by other villagers in struggles for more land and food supplies. As humans, we took the stance to fight for survival. We learnt how to speak with one another as well as fight in groups or couples. After the fights they would take stock of what they learned about fighting and then celebrate and socialize as a way taking the excess adrenaline and all the other hormones to a neutral function and not be stressed. This meant that they lived healthier lives.

Our Ancestors Fled

When our ancestors were out foraging through the forests and felt threatened by animals or other humans their response was to run. The adrenaline rush helped them increase their running speeds to hopefully avoid the threat. Each villager would run in a different direction, meaning that the threat had to pick a target to pursue. As with most hunters, they target the weak and lame so obviously the faster the villager ran, the less chance of being caught.

When it came to running away for survival, hormones were temporary. Often the villager had to find a clear path through tough terrain, recalling the best route to safety from their current location without drawing unnecessary attention The adrenaline helped them run for miles through thick forests, speed over empty deserts, and negotiate high cliffs, to safety. Their bodies used the excessive hormones pumping blood to the muscles for tackling obstacles.

Once the threat was gone, the group would come back together and find a place of safety to rest, count the survivors, eat and drink and celebrate their survival. After a good night's sleep, they were stress free and ready to run another day. This type of survival is what kept the human race going.

Our Ancestors Froze

Yes. It's true. Our ancestors sometimes froze in place and were eaten alive by the animals. Sometimes the fear of the threat is so great that our bodies just freeze.

Sometimes our flight or flee response doesn't kick in and we simply stay there like a deer in the headlights. Animals sometimes get so stressed they actually stay in place. They either get eaten alive, killed, or sometimes if they're lucky they're passed by unharmed

People go through that today. Sometimes they are so stressed out, that they are not sure what to do, that they freeze in place. They hold their breath, they scream, and practically stop breathing, and go into shock. After a while, once their body realizes that they're still alive, it returns to a functioning state. Normal breathing returns and the adrenaline rush dissipates.

Chapter 4: Impact of Stress on Health

Some of the most prevalent health concerns associated to stressful experiences include:

Accelerated Aging

Accelerated aging has always been an issue in discussions regarding stress. To provide facts regarding this issue, there have been various studies and research. There are various ways that stress can hasten the aging process in people:

Damage to Cells

This is due to workplace stress in our lives. By measuring the telomeres of different individuals, a study was able to determine that those with higher workplace stress levels had shorter telomere. The adverse effects associated with the shortening of the telomeres include cardiovascular diseases, Parkinson's, cancer, and type 2 diabetes.

It Ages the Brain

In another study by UC Berkeley, scientists identified that in females, higher stress levels could promote a rapid brain decline, which is aging-related.

Unhealthy Lifestyle Choices

Your habits have an effect on proper aging. Poor habits like sleep deprivation are a result of stress in your life. Sleep deprivation is one of the factors that promote rapid aging. It is also common to ignore exercises and don't eat a balanced diet while under stress. These individuals rely more on medications and alcohol. This will surely become noticeable in how the body ages.

Diabetes

Diabetes is another health issue that is affected and promoted by stress. In the people suffering from type 1 or type 2 diabetes, they suffer from the effects of physical stress. This form of stress causes a rise in the blood sugar level of the individual.

With mental stress, it might affect individuals with type 1 diabetes differently. For some, there will be an increase in blood glucose levels, while others will experience a decrease. For those with type 2 diabetes, there is also an issue when they are under mental stress. This type of stress results in a rise in the blood glucose level of the individual.

Stress can also promote diabetes. This is noticeable in the increase in the chances of an individual adopting lousy behavior. In this case, unhealthy food choices. They resort to excessive drinking and eating a poor diet. This might also affect those already suffering from this condition

Depression

Depression is one of the health issues that can result from chronic or acute stress. This situation occurs when the body is unable to shut-down and reset the stress response system after overcoming a stressful situation. A tasking job that offers minimal rewards or the loss of a loved one is one of such events.

Such events result in the reduction of neurotransmitters such as dopamine and serotonin, with an increase in cortisol levels. Due to the inability to shut-down the stress response, the body is unable to return these levels to normal, meaning that the body will be unable to function optimally.

This means there will be a dopamine deficiency in the body, which has a close link to depression in humans (Cadman & Falck, 2018). With lower stress levels, the risk of depression is much lower.

Obesity

Another significant health problem that individuals may experience due to stress is obesity. There has been researching with conclusions that prove this to be a fact. In one study, the samples used in determining this risk was the hair cortisol level (Whiteman, 2017).

According to this study, individuals with a higher hair cortisol level also had a heavier weight, bigger waist circumference, and more upper body mass index (BMI). In comparison to excess fat in the hips and leg area, excess belly fat poses a more significant health risk.

There is also the issue of "comfort eating," in which individuals try to make themselves feel better by consuming foods that have high sugar and fat content. This is an action that also promotes obesity, and this "comfort eating" is a result of stress.

Premature Death

If you don't manage stress properly, there is a high risk that it can shorten your lifespan. This includes the everyday stress you experience in life. Through chronic stress, there is a possibility of an increase in blood pressure.

Due to an increase in cortisol levels in the body, this type of stress lowers your immunity and affects your memory. In other situations, your reaction to everyday stress also has a role to play.

Heart Diseases

To establish a direct link between stress and heart diseases, there is a need for in-depth research into this area. Nonetheless, there are other indirect ways by which stress can lead to heart diseases.

There is a possibility of stress leading to heart muscle inflammation. This is one of the areas that play a role in heart diseases. The possibility of causing a sudden jump in your blood pressure is also present with stress.

People who experience stress tend to overeat, smoke, and drink. This is their solution to get over stress, but these actions also increase the risk of heart disease. There is also a risk of heart attack, hypertension, or stroke due to the damage to the blood vessel lining of an individual experiencing chronic stress.

Chapter 5:

When Stress Becomes Chronic

Experiencing short-lived stress is a normal part of our lives. However, if feelings of stress become long-lasting or chronic, then they can start to negatively impact a person's health. How can you tell when normal stress has passed into the unhealthy range?

As we learned in the second chapter, stress is part of the fight or flight response to help get the body ready for action. Once the moment that caused the stress passes, then the stress should go away too. However, chronic stress places pressure on the body for a long period of time. This can end up causing a range of symptoms and can even increase a person's risk of developing certain illnesses.

There are many people who let worrying and stress rule their day. Some new research has found that about 38 percent do worry during their day. Worry and its emotional sidekick, anger, feed the way we respond to create problem areas in life. They eat away at our ability to function at work and home.

Worrying too much could be deadly. It's possible that the next time someone tells you that their job is killing them, they're right. The good news is that we may develop resilience to shield ourselves against stressful events and the poisonous reactions they cause.

Signs of Chronic Stress

Chronic stress will affect the entire body. There are a number of psychological or physical symptoms that can occur when you experience chronic stress, which can create problems in your daily life. The severity of the symptoms, and the type of symptoms, can vary for each person.

1. *Acne – Acne is a physical sign that stress is causing problems.*

When people start to feel stressed out, they tend to touch their faces a lot. This ends up spreading bacteria and can contribute to acne popping up. A lot of studies have found that acne is linked to higher stress levels. There was a study that looked at acne severity in 22 people before and during an exam. Higher stress levels because of exam stress caused more acne. Besides excess stress, another reason for acne due to stress is hormonal shifts, blocked pores, excess oil production, and bacteria.

2. *Headaches – Chronic headaches can be a side effect of chronic stress.*

A lot of studies have found that stress can contribute to headaches, which are any form of pain felt in the neck or head area. A study looked at 267 people who suffered from chronic headaches.

They all said that a stressful event would often precede the development of a headache in 45 percent of cases.

3. *Chronic Pain – Random pains and aches are common complaints from those who experience* a lot of stress.

There are studies that have found that increased levels of cortisol are connected to chronic pain. They studied a group of 16 persons who had chronic back pain in one trial. Compared to the control group, those with chronic pain tended to have higher cortisol levels. They also discovered that persons who suffer from chronic pain have greater cortisol levels in their hair, which is an excellent predictor of long-term stress.

4. *Frequent illnesses or infections – If you always feel like you are dealing with the sniffles, it could be stress.*

Stress really affects the immune system, which increases your risk of infections. There was one study that took 61 people and gave them the flu vaccine. Of those who had chronic stress, they were found to have a weakened immune response, which meant that stress could cause a decrease in immunity. However, it's important to understand that stress is only one thing that affects immune health.

- Insomnia and Decreased Energy – If you always feel tired and have low energy levels, it can be due to prolonged stress.

In a study of 2,483 people, they found that fatigue had a strong connection to increased stress levels. Stress can also end up interrupting your sleep, which also makes you feel even more tired.

- Changes in Libido – There are a lot of people who experience a change in their sex drives when in a stressful situation.

A study of 30 women measured their arousal while watching erotic films. The women who had higher levels of chronic stress were not as easily aroused as those with lower stress levels.

- Digestive Problems – It is common for stress to cause issues like constipation and diarrhea.

In a study of 2,699 children, researchers discovered that those who were exposed to stressful conditions had a higher chance of constipation. Stress can also affect those who have digestive disorders like IBS.

- Appetite Changes – It's very common for people to experience appétit changes when stressed.

When a person is stressed, they may discover that they don't have much of an appetite, or they are extremely hungry and constantly go snacking. A study of students discovered that 81 percent of them had experienced some type of change in appetite whenever they became stressed. Of those who had experienced changes, 62 percent saw an increase in appetite, while 38 percent had a decrease in appetite. There was a study of 129 people that found that being exposed to stress was connected to the act of eating when not actually hungry.

- Depression – There are studies that have found that chronic stress could contribute to the development of depression.

One study looked at 816 women who had major depression and discovered that the onset of the depression had a strong connection with chronic and acute stress. There was yet another study that found that high levels of stress were connected with higher levels of depression symptoms. Plus, there was a study with 38 people who had non-chronic major depression that discovered that stressful moments in life were connected with depressive episodes. Keep in mind that these studies do show a connection, but it does not mean that stress causes depression.

Some other symptoms of chronic stress can include:

- Nervousness
- Low self-esteem
- A perceived loss of control
- Feeling helpless
- Disorganized, rapid thoughts
- Difficulty concentrating
- Irritability

Worry and Stress

A big factor in stress becoming chronic is worry. Here are some signs that you might be worrying too much and ways you can get rid of this worry before it gets out of control:

- You Are Always Looking for Threats

You have probably created a habit of reacting to certain evens anxiously. This is known as the "fear of future threats." This mentality will take over our thinking, and we will interpret every single thing as a possible problem. We will constantly be looking for threats, and this turns us into worriers.

There is a way to fix this. You have to separate your anxiety from what is happening right now. Are you catastrophizing about it, or is it a worst-case scenario? You have to quit confusing, anxious feelings with an actual reason for you to worry.

- You Aren't Able to Sleep

Not getting enough sleep means you won't be able to emotionally function properly, and this, in turn, will lead to even more stress, and this promotes worse sleep. It just keeps creating vicious cycle after vicious cycle.

There is a way to fix this. If you want to interrupt the cycle, get out of bed an hour earlier. You have to turn the night into a safe place where your daily stressors can't live. Rather than looking at your phone or tablet until your eyes can't stay open, begin putting all electronics away one hour before you go to bed. This will get rid of all temptations and distractions. What can you do if you feel guilty about unwinding? You have to remind yourself that getting a good night's sleep is the best foundation for being able to function properly. You will be able to handle all of life's challenges the next day. You have to give yourself permission to shut everything off, including yourself. This will be the best thing for you in the long run. Keep in mind that sleep is not something that is expendable.

- You Can't Quit Feeling Upset

Everyone has felt that prickly, jarring sensation after we've had a bad encounter. These aftershocks can last a very long time. You constantly relive it and wonder if there were things, we might have been able to do differently. We replay this over and over again while second-guessing the way we responded.

You can fix this by getting up and moving. Anytime you feel like you are trapped and are replaying what happened, leave. Wherever you are at this moment, just walk away. If you are in the middle of grocery shopping, leave your shopping cart where it's at and walk outside. If you are at work, leave whatever you are doing and go outside to take a short walk around the block. You will be able to go back feeling refreshed and stronger. Hopefully, your shopping cart will be where you left it, but if not, no big deal, just get another one and start again. Once you have freed yourself from the stressful mindset, you will be able to make better decisions. Once you have reset your mind and body, do a check-in: "Was the situation as bad as you thought it was?" "Was it worth getting so upset over?" Most of the time, you are going to answer no to both questions.

- You Begin Feeling Resentful

We all expect other people to be able to read our minds. This is the best way to feel disappointed all the time. You have been caught up in what most psychologists like to call a "mind-reading trap." This can cause all sorts of disagreements and resentment since your expectations are not realistic.

You can fix this by stopping expecting others to be able to know what you need. You have to ask for help if you need it. If you don't feel like you are in the loop or you feel like things are out of your control, quit getting angry and speak up. Talk to your coworkers or employees. If they aren't doing what you asked them to do, were you clear on your instructions? Did you tell them exactly what you wanted and when you needed it done? You have to learn how to communicate properly.

- You Get Overrun by Guilt

You've asked your boss for a raise that you believe you deserve, and now you're worried about offending him. You took credit for a project that was a success; then, you begin feeling guilty for all the attention you are getting. If guilt is your default emotion, you will begin looking at positive things through a worry lens, and then you feel like you have violated other people's rights.

You can fix this by challenging your thoughts. Is what you are feeling warranted. Are you fixated on things that aren't there? The following are some questions you should ask yourself: "How much do I believe I owe this individual, and would I expect them to repay me?" If that's the case, what's the point of the double standard?"

You would not have gotten mad if one of your employees asked you for a raise or they claimed credit for a well-done project, so you need to give yourself the same benefits.

Chapter 6:

What You Think, Matters

Stress may manifest itself in physical ways, but it's very much a psychological issue. Your mind can produce negative thoughts and create anxiety and tension, affecting you physically and psychologically. If you choose to, you can think yourself out of this negative state of being.

Living under stress and pressure is a common way of living in the modern day. This often reflects itself in thinking negatively and trying to be perfect, chasing far-away goals, or creating a lifestyle that requires high maintenance and lots of hard work.

Stress is created inside the mind even before a stressful event occurs. And the self-talk that follows a stressful event is not helpful either.

Please answer the following questions:

- Do you often feel you are too tough on yourself and don't show much compassion towards your needs and feelings?

- Do you speak to yourself as if you are your own worst enemy and rarely use positive and encouraging language when speaking to yourself?

- Do you congratulate yourself on putting out your best effort?

Can you see how stress can be self-imposed? Your negative self-talk and lack of self-care can create internal turmoil that will not only affect your inner world but will negatively impact your outside world too.

Negative thoughts and discouraging language only act to embolden and bolster negativity. However, thinking positively and using positive self-talk can bring about beneficial, positive changes and create new opportunities.

You Are What You Think

This book focuses on the seven strategies that yielded great results when working with my clients, helping them to handle their stress in positive ways.

Learning to think positively and developing positive self-talk are the most important aspects of stress management, and they cannot be ignored. They are the foundation on which all other coping strategies are built.

If you tell yourself something enough times, you will start believing in it. The majority of us have the problem of not often telling ourselves positive things. This leads to creating a negative mindset.

Lack of positivity can affect your self-esteem and confidence levels. To create a healthy balance, you need to focus on the way you think and develop a belief system that works in your favor.

If you keep saying to yourself, "I'm fat", "I'm ugly", "I'm too loud", "I'm no good at this job", "I'm never going to be able to do this", it can negatively affect your confidence and bring additional stress into your life.

The mind-body link is critical for your health, and you should never underestimate its strength or how it impacts you. A healthy relationship between your mind and body can help you connect to your inner strength and overcome negativity from the outside world. On the other hand, if your mind-body connection is broken and not serving you well, your well-being will suffer, impacting your stress levels, amongst other things.

Did you know that most of your thinking is automatic?

Your voice greatly influences your mind. Your self-critical voice can affect your thought process and behavior much more than your external circumstances.

A good starting point to change your way of thinking is to identify patterns in your everyday self-talk. This is not something you can change quickly, and you should not expect to see results overnight. Most of your thought-patterns and self-talk are ingrained in you. Therefore, giving yourself time to recognize the issue, reframe it in your mind, and repeat it until it becomes second nature will take time. You must be patient. You owe it to yourself. Remember that!

Some of the thoughts you have might not seem negative or evident at first, but that is where your stress journal will come in handy. If these thoughts keep reappearing in your subconscious mind, it's a good indication that they are an issue, and you need to act on them accordingly. Tracking everything in your journal that produces stress, and recording all your negative thoughts throughout the day, will bring clarity and understanding.

Here are some of the thoughts that might be causing you to feel stressed — thoughts you might not be aware of:

- I should never make mistakes
- I make too many mistakes
- People don't like me
- I'm not as good as others
- I have to do my job perfectly all the time
- I need to keep proving myself to others so they can accept me
- I will never get it right
- I need to be the best, otherwise people will not respect me
- If someone gives me feedback or criticism, it means I have done something wrong

- I need to please other people, otherwise they will not like me
- I am the way I am, and I cannot change how I think
- No one cares about me
- I know I'm going to fail at this; I never succeed in anything
- I should never show my weaknesses
- I need to control everything around me
- I don't understand why others don't see things the way I do
- If they loved me, they would do as I ask
- The world is a cruel and unfair place

These thoughts are your self-limiting beliefs. They are your biggest enemy. And they can affect your life more than you can imagine. However, with practice, you can learn ways to boost your mind and body connection.

Here are some ideas that I think you should try:

- Write down your thoughts – The first suggestion is to use your stress journal and add all your daily thoughts to your notes, whether positive or negative. This can be an excellent way to seek clarity, but it also tracks what you are thinking and how often it occupies your mind.
- Don't be afraid to ask for help – Many people find it hard to ask for help and feel that it will make them look weak

and needy. Therefore, they prefer to go it alone. But in reality, seeking help can make you a stronger person.

- Make sure you address any problems or worries you have – Stress often occurs when we push our thoughts and feelings to one side and try to ignore them. If you have a recurrent type of worry, make sure you write it in your journal and track how often it bothers you. You're providing yourself the information you need to address the problem by doing so.

- Relax! – We all need a little chill-out time occasionally. Always running around and trying to fix every problem will tire you out mentally and physically, forcing more negativity into your life. Make sure that you place a considerable amount of importance on self-care and relaxation. Find out what relaxes you, and then do more of it.

- Understand the sensations you feel and what they mean – Do you feel a little short of breath when you are worried? Do you feel lightheaded when you panic? Do you feel stressed around the same time each day? Learn to recognize how emotions make you feel and try to connect them with different events. By doing this, you can preempt situations and use deep breathing exercises (more on those shortly) to help you reconnect and overcome the peak emotion. Understanding your feelings can help you with strengthening your mind-body connection.

- Acknowledge your negativity – If you have negative thoughts, try not to run away from them as you won't succeed in escaping them. Instead, acknowledge how you feel, what you are thinking, and place a name and label on it. Awareness of your thoughts will give you the power to change them.

The Art of Mindfulness and How It Can Benefit You

There is a buzz around the word mindfulness at the moment. Mindfulness helps develop a more positive mindset, create inner peace, increase happiness and contentment, and bring awareness to the present moment.

This strategy works very well when working on reducing stress, and I will talk about it throughout the rest of this book.

As humans, we have a proclivity to be concerned about the future or to bemoan the loss of memories from the past. When we do that, we are not living in the moment. We are missing out. Mindfulness helps us keep our feet firmly on the ground by giving us control of the present moment and giving us chance to connect to ourselves. The moment we live in is the only time we can control, and mindfulness keeps us grounded and safe in the present. This can have tremendous benefits for our emotional well-being and state of mind, helping us feel more at peace with our everyday stressors.

Now, let's look at the main benefit of practicing mindfulness to help you understand the power of living in the moment and the effects that it can have on you.

The benefits of mindfulness:

- The ability to live in the now and therefore cultivate stronger and healthier relationships with other people and yourself

- Being completely absorbed in what you're doing

- Being able to savour life's pleasures as you encounter them

- A more positive and happier mindset

- The ability to deal with life's lemons and truly turn them into lemonade

- The ability to observe events in life, allowing them to unfold as they are meant to, without judgment or pressure to change things.

- The ability to worry far less and reduce the chance of developing anxiety and depression

- A reduced chance of developing mental health issues, such as obsessive-compulsive disorder and eating disorders

- Increased confidence and self-worth

- Stress relief

- Lowered blood pressure, which helps to reduce the risk of developing cardiovascular issues, such as heart disease

- Relief from chronic pain

- A better night's sleep

- Relief from regular gastrointestinal issues, often related to stress

Practicing mindfulness can give you all these benefits and help you to be calmer and happier. It will reduce your stress and the tendency to worry excessively.

When you first try mindfulness, you might struggle with it a little bit. Not being an expert in something which you have never tried before is perfectly normal. By practicing mindfulness regularly, you will begin to see the benefits.

Try this:

- Choose a spot — a place that feels quiet and calm.
- Set a time — dedicate a specific time for mindfulness each day.
- Choose a comfortable position — you can sit or lie down. Do what feel relaxed, comfortable, and natural to you.
- Notice your breathing patterns — breathe in slowly through your nose and exhale through your mouth.
- Notice when your mind wanders — acknowledge it, accept it, and allow it to pass through your mind and back out again.

I suggest that you practice a mindfulness meditation exercise daily. With mindfulness, the more you put into it, the more you will get out of it.

Using the deep breathing exercise to deal with peak emotional experiences, for instance, when you notice your stress starting to rise, can be a great stress release.

Begin each day with a mindfulness meditation session, and you will set the tone for the rest of the day. This will increase your chances of linking your mind and body.

There are other ways you can utilize mindfulness in your daily routine. Here are some examples:

- When you are eating, focus on chewing your food. You will notice the taste and feel the texture of the food. You will most probably realize that your mind doesn't wander during this time; instead, it focuses on the present moment and enjoys what you are consuming.

- The next time you are at the gym, out for a walk, jogging, or swimming, try doing a mindfulness exercise. Notice how your body feels with every movement. Observe how your muscles contract and give you the power to move forwards. Pay attention to each breath and how it gives you energy as you go through the motions.

9 Ways Mindfulness Can Reduce Stress

I have talked a lot about mindfulness and how it can help you be more positive and present in the moment, but how does all of this help with stress management, you may wonder? Let's look into this now.

1. Your thoughts can create stress inside your body – Mindfulness allows you to be more aware of your thoughts and the feelings you have about those thoughts. Understanding this can create awareness and will enable you to deal with your emotions more positively.

2. Practicing mindfulness allows you to stop and take stock of the situation and keep everything in perspective – I'm sure you are aware of the danger of acting upon an issue without giving much thought to it beforehand. Acting when stressed can initiate even more stress. Mindfulness will prevent you from doing this.

3. Mindfulness helps you relax – It keeps you in the "being" mode instead of the "doing" mode. Feeling the need to do something continuously is likely to make you stressed. When you practice mindfulness, your mind is more relaxed. And when you know how to relax, stress is not as much of a problem.

4. Mindfulness makes you more aware of the connection between the mind and body and how your mental state affects your physical state – Knowing this helps you be more in charge of your physical health. You can sit down and take a few deep breaths, or you can go outside and move your body. This will alter your thoughts and feelings.

5. Mindfulness increases your emotional intelligence (EQ) – Mindfulness makes you more connected to your mind and

body as one, and when you have a high EQ level, you will find it easier to side-step the things that don't really matter. People with higher EQ (nothing to do with IQ) can prioritize the actions worth acting upon and downplay the importance of actions that have less value.

6. Mindfulness makes you more compassionate and aware – As your EQ grows, your ability to act kindly to yourself and others increases. You are less prone to suffer stress on a regular basis if this occurs.

7. Mindfulness enhances your ability to focus on the task at hand – For example, many people become stressed at work. It is one of the most common stressors. However, mindfulness can help you to focus on one thing at a time far better than you would without the application of mindfulness. As a result, you will not feel quite so stressed because your focus will be sharper, enhancing your productivity level.

8. Mindfulness reframes your stress-related attitude – When you become more mindful, you will understand that stress is merely a response to something which may or may not be a real issue, and you will be able to manage your situation better.

9. Mindfulness reduces stress by working on the amygdala – The amygdala is a part of your brain which is heavily associated with emotions and, as a result, it is one of the

critical aspects of the brain that concerns stress. Our emotions cause stress to rise, so working on this part of the brain naturally reduces stress.

As you can see, becoming more conscious of your internal story and confronting it in general has no disadvantages. Mindfulness can help you create inner peace and help you choose one thought over another so that you can feel more in charge of your emotional, mental, and physical well-being.

Developing a Positive Mindset

There are many aspects of life that we have no control over. But you are always in control of your own thoughts. You have a choice of what you want to focus on and how you will react to it.

"If you change the way you look at things, the things you look at change," Wayne Dyer stated.

You will live a life free of stress and anxiety, with more tranquility and quiet in its place, if you choose to focus on the positive.

A positive mindset enables you to feel happier and handle stress more easily. Of course, if you have developed a habit of thinking negatively for many years, it will not be a smooth ride, but the saying "practice makes perfect" applies to this.

A positive mindset will allow you to see the glass as half-full rather than half-empty. It will encourage you to look for the silver linings rather than automatically jumping towards doom and gloom.

Developing a positive mindset takes time, but the more you practice, the more you will notice the changes in your mood, and your outlook on life will take a different shape. You will feel happier, healthier, and more positive. You will notice many opportunities coming your way because you will be open to them and feel more confident in taking them on. This will result in overcoming challenges and problems that can noticeably reduce your stress levels.

A few ways to start working on developing a positive mindset include:

- Start the day with a positive affirmation – Make sure you choose words that resonate with you. For instance, "today, I am positive and strong", "I believe everything will work out for me" or "I will not stress over things I cannot control". There are many affirmations to choose from if you check online, or you can make up your own. Repeat your affirmations three times in the morning as soon as you wake up and repeat them whenever you feel a need to hear them throughout the day. Remember, the more you tell yourself something, the more you believe in it!

- Focus on the good things – Life is full of ups and downs, and certain situations will always make you feel bad. But there is a light in every shadow, and positives are hiding in all the negatives. If you look for a silver lining, you will always find it.

- Finding humor in the darkest of situations – Laughter is one of the best medicines. It can turn any situation around on its head and help you see that nothing is quite as bad as it first seems.

- Turn mistakes into lessons – When you make a mistake, look at how you could do it differently next time and learn from it. If something goes wrong, find a lesson within it.

- Reframe your negative thoughts – Nothing in life is good or bad; it's your perception of the situation that makes it that way. Certain things or people became your stressors only because you let them.

- Practice mindfulness – Mindfulness can not only benefit your health, but it can also help you develop a more positive mindset and enable you to stay in the present moment, rather than focus on the past's negative experiences or fears about the future.

- Surround yourself with positive people – If a person from your inner circle is draining your energy, it is fair to say that your health and life are likely to be affected. It may sound harsh, but you need to leave this person behind and move on to a brighter future without them. The quality of your life depends on your surroundings and the people you spend most of your time with. Some people will push you forwards, and others will pull you backwards. Make sure you choose to share your life only with people who will move you forwards and lift you higher.

3 Ways to Manage Negative Thoughts

Negativity is the human default mind setting. On average, we have around 60,000 thoughts a day. Most of them are repetitive, and a large percentage of them are negative.

Learning to control harmful and unhelpful thoughts and turn them into beneficial ones will help you develop a healthier and more positive mindset.

There are several methods of controlling negative thoughts, including thought stopping, replacing negative thoughts with more helpful ideas, and reframing.

Here is how they work in practice:

Thought Stopping

Thought stopping is a beneficial method to help you control negative thoughts. It might seem impossible at first to stop yourself from having unwanted thoughts and ideas, but with practice and with an open mind, you will find that it becomes much easier over time.

When using this technique, it is important to recognize your negative thoughts and acknowledge them. Give yourself three minutes to focus on this thought and say "Stop!" out loud. You might find it useful to visualize pushing the thoughts away with your hand. If you notice the thought returning, say "Stop!" once again. Repeat this process until the negative thought has gone.

This particular technique is very effective, and the more you practice, the easier it will become to handle your negative thoughts and enable you to push them away.

Replacing

Another way of controlling your thoughts is to replace a negative thought with a happy one, and distract yourself with something you like doing and find fun. The more you focus on the happier thought, the unwanted thought will have less space in your mind. The reason why this method works is because we cannot feel positive and negative at the same time, and we cannot be stressed and relaxed at the same time. One condition will have to prevail and win over the other.

Reframing

In the previous chapter, I mentioned a technique called reframing. This is a cognitive behavioral therapy technique, often referred to as CBT. Reframing can be used in various situations, and over time, it can change your thought process from a negative into a positive.

This is how reframing works:

- Acknowledge that you are having a negative thought and label it as negatives in your mind.
- Turn the negative into a positive. For example, if you think, "I hate commuting to work for an hour every day. It takes lots of my energy and so much of my time", turn this into a positive and say, "I love commuting to work for an hour

every day. I'm using this time to relax and read a book while travelling on a train." Can you see how reframing can make a big difference to your state of mind?

- Repeat the new thought and visualize yourself sitting on a train and reading a book, feeling relaxed.

- Whenever you are rushing to work in the morning or travelling back home after a long day, bring this new thought to your mind — imagine yourself sitting on the train, reading an inspiring book, and feeling grateful and calm while reflecting on the positive aspects of your life.

- Over time, the positive will replace the negative.

As with many mindset exercises, reframing relies upon repetition. This is how the brain learns.

If you think back to when you were at school, you can probably remember singing the alphabet song over and over again until it stuck in your mind. Your teacher kept asking you to repeat it as they were trying to implant the alphabet deep into your subconscious via repetition.

Repetition is vital for your brain to remember things, whether positive or negative.

Your subconscious mind is like a sponge. It absorbs all the good and bad experiences from your life and remembers all the helpful and unhelpful words you say to yourself. Repetition will go through the filter surrounding your subconscious mind much more effortlessly than occasional occurrences. The more you repeat the stories and experiences that have some meaning to you, the more chance they will stay there. These thoughts will remain in your subconscious mind and affect every aspect of your life until they get replaced with other recurring events or words you tell yourself.

When repeated enough times, your subconscious mind accepts your thoughts as truth, and that's how you become what you think. Your thoughts affect your emotions and influence your behavior. They can make you feel happy or sad, stressed or relaxed, anxious or calm. And by forcing yourself to think more happily and positively, you will become more optimistic and positive by default.

This is how all your habits are born. The only way to develop any kind of habit is through repetition. When you do something again and over again, it becomes a learned behavior, which eventually becomes a routine. When this happens, you do things on auto-pilot.

Think of your morning routine. You probably get up in the morning on the same side of the bed as you did the day before. Then you most likely use the bathroom, brush your teeth, get dressed, have breakfast, etc. Your morning routine might follow a slightly different order, but you get the idea.

Most of your daily activities are led by your routines and influenced by your habits. The mind behaves the same way.

When you repeat your thoughts enough times, they become habits — a learned behavior that dictates all your feelings and actions. When this happens, they take control of your inner and outer world.

The good news is, you can take charge of the situation and change your thought process. This will help you enhance your mental, emotional, and physical health while also lowering your stress levels.

Chapter 7:

A Step-By-Step Guide to Tackling Stress Head-On

The best way to handle stressful situations is to be prepared. While there are many stressful situations you could never foresee or expect, there are lots of common situations causing full-blown panic attacks, overeating, and heart palpitations.

It might feel silly, but writing down the scenarios that usually cause anxiety and stress in your life will help you cope better in those specific situations. Note down the steps you can take to handle those situations better, thereby, reducing the impact that stress has on your body and quality of life.

Let's consider a few of these.

The Dire Work Deadline Meltdown

So, you wake up one morning in quite a good mood, go off to work with your latte in hand, turn on your computer and find, as you choke on your last sip, that you have a nine-o clock deadline in which you have to submit your annual report to your boss.

While the easy solution to this dilemma is to type out an annual report in an hour, this is ineffective and likely not your best work.

The Less Stress Solution

- Take a deep breath and acknowledge that you were wrong. It happens. It's ok. You might get into trouble, you might not. Either way the best way to create less stress in this situation is to fix the situation in the best way possible.

- Consider your options: Is there a portion of the work that can be done before your deadline, enabling you to provide your boss with at least some helpful information?

- Consider how you will make a bad situation look just a tad bit better. It is definitely not advisable to tell your boss you missed your deadline because you were too busy Skyping while at work (and if this is true you will be able to reduce your stress simply by eliminating non-work-related distractions during working hours).

- Speak to your boss. This is likely the last thing you want to do, but it will be a critical step toward finding a solution. Your boss might be able to give you some extra time to complete the report or even offer to assist you. Or your boss might go all red, yell at you and threaten to fire you if this happens again. In either instance, the most important thing is that you handle the situation professionally and show your manager that you are willing to apologize.

- Breathe and reflect. The best way to overcome a really stressful situation that results from a mistake is by assuring yourself that you will not do it again and reflecting on why it happened in the first place.

The Embarrassing Temper Tantrum Touchdown

If you have experienced one of those embarrassing public temper tantrums before, you probably have a child (or a very immature spouse) and have found yourself bright red in a grocery store or a mall considering whether you should run and leave your child for a stranger to raise or pretend he's not yours.

The Less Stress Solution

- Maintain your composure regardless of how furious or embarrassed you are. Try to take a few deep breaths (yes, it is hard to do that while your toddler's screams pierce through your mind).

- Create a diversion. You know best what will divert your child's attention away from the current situation. Instead of rewarding negative behavior with a negative response focus his attention on something else.

- Have 'the talk' when you get home. Only once your toddler has calmed down, explain to him why his behavior was not acceptable and how you expect him to behave in future – use positive reinforcement.

- Be prepared. Next time you go to the mall or to a shop tell your toddler that there will be an excellent reward at home for good behavior and constantly remind him of this.

The Mother of all mother-in-Law Situations

Your mother-in-law phones and announces that she will be coming to stay with you for a while – quite a long while. Naturally, in the midst of work deadlines, school activities and personal to do lists that never seem to get done you are a second away from losing your mind.

The Less Stress Solution

- Put yourself in her shoes. You will also be a mother (or father) in law one day and would want to spend time at your son or daughter's house and be a part of their family.

- Try and make the best of the situation. Think about your to-do list and how you can tick some of those points off while your mother-in-law is at your house. Try to hand over some of your responsibilities to her.

- Just let it be. She will not be there forever so if she wants to take over the cooking or fold the towels differently just let her. You can always refold as soon as she is out the door.

- Find the best approach to talk to her about it if the matter gets out of hand and you feel like she's taking over your home. Put yourself in her shoes and think about how you would like someone to approach you in a similar situation.

The Breakdown Break

While we all love a break it usually comes as a nasty surprise when you get an unexpected one in your car. Car breakdowns are one of the most unpleasant circumstances you can encounter because they usually occur when you are finishing a task or, in the worst-case scenario, on your way to work.

The Less Stress Solution

- Relax and stop thinking about the fact that you might be holding up traffic or that people are looking at you. Yes, they are looking at you, but chances are that at least two out of three people passing you by have been in the same situation.

- Take charge of the aspects of your life that you have control over. Either phone emergency roadside assistance or phone a friend.

- Call the person or company you were on your way to see and explain to them what happened. Tell them that you will reschedule your appointment as soon as you are able to.

- "Why does this have to happen to me?" In a horrible scenario, this is one of the most frequently asked questions. Do not take it personally. Realize that while you are sitting in your broken-down car there are people in much worse situations and you are lucky to even have a car. You might not feel like being grateful at that moment but putting things into perspective can help. A lot. Have some support.

Get a friend on the phone or on instant chat and speak to them – even though they can't be there in real time it will make you feel less alone.

- Accept that you cannot change the situation. Even if you were on your way to an important meeting, you surely could not have foreseen the fact that your car would break down.

- Take a well-deserved break in a bad situation. Sit in your car and wait for assistance and use this time to reflect – something we never seem to have time for.

The Overabundance of Sick Children and Absence of Babysitters Bash

If you are a parent and you are employed full time you might have experienced this one before; you're busy at work. Extremely busy. You get a call from your child's school saying she's sick and that you need to take her up immediately away. You first panic, wondering what is wrong with your child, and then panic at the thought of having to tell your boss you need to leave the office.

You swing into full-fledged babysitter finding mode but despite your best efforts can't find anyone to go and get your baby.

The Less Stress Solution

- Realize that your family always comes first and you do not have to apologize for that.

- Consider that your boss also has a family and while he or she has a lot of stress to deal with at work and might get a tad bit annoyed at you having to leave, they understand deep down that having a sick child is not a choice.

- Tell your boss that you will work from home if possible and keep him or her updated.

- Stop feeling guilty for leaving to take care of your sick child – your number one job is being a parent and you should never feel guilty about that. Employers know that they hire people, not machines.

- To feel less guilty about having to take time off, thank your boss for understanding when you get back to work and tell them that you will catch up on any missed work as soon as possible.

The Spousal Miscommunication Mayhem

You have been stuck inside with a screaming baby all day and your husband come home after working late and gets upset because there is nothing to eat.

The Less Stress Solution

- Even though you are currently bone-tired, lacking in grown up conversation and frustrated, take a few seconds to consider your spouse's day before you go into a full-blown meltdown.

- Consider that you are not in the right frame of mind to speak about the fact that your spouse was just a tad bit

- insensitive. Rather ask him to make something for himself or to order in.

- When you both feel better (spouses' tummy is full, you had a long hot bath and are relaxed in front of the TV) tell your spouse that you had a hard day and that, even though you are at home all day while he is at work, you find it hard to cope sometimes and will not always be able to have dinner ready. Inquire about how you and he can collaborate to ensure that you can eat meals together at night and unwind following a long day.

- Do not explode if he does not offer an apology immediately for being insensitive – instead think about the fact that you are took a stressful situation and turned it into a normal conversation.

The Asking for Money Madness

This seems to be an awkward situation all around. No one like asking for money as, in most cases, we feel it should not be asked for; if a friend borrowed money from you, it should be obvious that he should pay it back. If you worked for someone, you should have been paid upon project approval. If you are taking on more responsibility at work and performing well, you expect your boss to see it and reward you accordingly.

All of this is correct…in an ideal world. But people forget, or don't notice or simply don't have the money to pay what they owe.

The Less Stress Solution

If you Need to Confront Someone that Owes you Money:

- Just don't be awkward. By acting awkward when you ask someone for your money you are making them feel awkward in return. Just be straight up, relaxed and remember to smile.

- Be firm but nice. Make the person understand that you need the money for your own personal situation.

- If you realize that the person is unable to pay you back offer to work out a payment plan.

- Follow these procedures if you need to approach your manager for a raise.

- Be prepared. You can't ask for a raise if you don't have good reasons and some factual evidence of why you deserve one.

- Be sure to let your employer know that you are thankful for the opportunity to work for him or her and that you look forward to growing in the company.

- Don't bring your personal life to the table. The fact that you just had twins or need to look after your mother-in-law has nothing to do with your company and is not a good reason to ask for a raise. Only work-related results are.

- Be professional. If your boss notes that he is unable to give you a raise now, ask when in future it would be possible and what you can do to make the decision easier.

- Don't leave things unresolved. If your boss was unable to give you answer, ask if you can setup a follow-up meeting in which you can discuss his or her decision.

The Pubic Presentation Perspiration Situation

Your stomach has been in knots for days, your palms keep sweating and whenever you rehearse the presentation, you're supposed to give in front of the whole company in three days your voice starts shaking uncontrollably.

The Less Stress Solution

- Prepare, prepare and prepare some more. Being prepared will make you feel less nervous. Better yet, actually understanding the topic you will be presenting will enable you to speak from the heart instead of sounding like you are reading from a book.

- Get the audience involved. By adding a joke that everyone in the company knows or asking specific members of the audience a question will help to place the attention on other people and not make you feel so isolated.

- Breathe. The best way to keep your composure and voice from shaking is by ensuring good breathing techniques. When setting up your presentation, make sure you add pauses into the content – places where you can draw the audience's attention to something else while you gulp some air and steady yourself.

- Rehearse your presentation in front of as many people as possible. Even though you might feel silly while doing it – that is the whole point. The more comfortable you can get with being uncomfortable the better.

Chapter 8:

Managing a Stressed Brain

Effective stress management may free you from the shackles of stress, allowing you to live a healthier, happier, and more productive life. What we desire is a healthy balance of relationships, work, play, and relaxation, as well as the ability to persevere when things become rough. There are numerous ways for stress management, some of which may or may not work for you. That is why it is crucial to experiment and figure out what works best for you.

Let's debunk some myths about stress before we move forward.

- Stress is all around you, and there is nothing you can do about it.

True, stress is all around us, but you can manage your life such that it does not consume you. Setting priorities and fixing basic problems first before tackling more complex challenges is a good technique. When we are stressed, it is difficult to prioritize because all concerns appear to be equally distressing.

- Only the most serious stress symptoms need to be addressed.

Minor signals of an out-of-control life, such as headaches or stomach acid, should not be ignored. Do not wait until a serious stress symptom, e.g., a heart attack, to get help; it may already be too late. Making lifestyle changes such as increasing your physical activity or eating a healthier diet will save you time, money, and enhance your health. Furthermore, if symptoms are not controlled, stress can quickly progress from acute to chronic.

- Stress can be used as a motivator.

Although some people are motivated by stress, the benefits of motivation do not exceed the overall detrimental impact on health. Chinese community health professionals were asked about their work stress and motivation in connection to job satisfaction in a 2014 poll. This study discovered that work-related stress had a negative relationship with job satisfaction using two separate criteria.

Short-term stress, particularly acute stress, can be motivating for some people. Acute stress improves an individual's alertness and helps them complete tasks such as reaching key deadlines. Acute stress may also assist people in performing at their best and thinking imaginatively about how to overcome difficulties. Stress is justified as a motivator in some situations.

Chronic stress, however, which has long-term negative consequences, is less of a motivator and more of a burden. The long-term disadvantages of chronic stress on a person's physical, mental, and emotional well-being outweighs the benefits of acute stress.

- If there are no signs or symptoms, there is no stress.

Just because a person does not exhibit stress-related signs or symptoms does not indicate that they are not stressed. Stress can quickly manifest itself in some people through behavioral changes or after traumatic occurrences. However, it may be incredibly difficult to tell if some are stressed, based on their conduct. Such people may appear normal and hide their tension successfully, but they are undoubtedly battling emotionally. Stress is usually manifested in two ways: cognitively and emotionally.

The following stress management methods can assist you in your stress-free journey:

Identifying Source of Stress

Exploring the reasons behind your stressed life is the primary step in stress management. However, figuring them out might not be straightforward. While major stresses such as moving, changing jobs, or going through a divorce are obvious, identifying the causes of chronic stress can be challenging. It is easy to misunderstand the part that your own feelings, ideas, and behaviors have in your stress levels. You may be continually worried about work deadlines, but it is possible that the stress is caused by your procrastination instead of the actual job obligations.

Examine your actions, attitudes, and justifications to determine your true stressors:

- Do you consider stress to be a part of your employment or personal life ("Things are often a little frenetic around here") or a personality attribute ("I simply have a lot of worried energy, that's all")?

- Do you rationalize your stress as transient ("I just have a million things on my plate right now"), despite the fact that you cannot recall the last time you took a break?

- Do you think your stress is caused due to other people or external circumstances, or do you think it is completely unexceptional and typical?

Your stress will stay out of your control unless you accept responsibility for your part in causing or perpetuating it.

Keeping a Stress Journal Will Help You Understand Your Problem

Keeping a notebook or diary is more than just a tool to record your ideas and experiences. Journaling is an effective stress alleviation practice, according to recent studies, and those who write in a diary or other notebook receive both physical and emotional advantages, perhaps extending their lives.

When compared to a control group, psychotherapy patients who were told to express their emotions through expressive writing had lower anxiety and depression symptoms and made more progress in psychotherapy, according to a recent study published in Psychotherapy Research.

Journaling may also assist you in reducing the amount of worry you experience. Another study published in the journal Behavior Modification found that expressive writing was linked to significant reductions in symptoms of generalized anxiety disorder, such as depression and worry.

How to do it?

Some people find putting pen to paper to be therapeutic, while others prefer typing their thoughts into a computer. There are even Web sites that allow people to journal privately online, such as LiveJournal and Penzu.

Take some time for yourself in a peaceful, comfortable location where you will not be disturbed. Simply start writing and date your journal entry. When it comes to journaling, there are no hard and fast rules. You can write anything that you want. You can make your diary entry as long or as short as you choose. Because no one but you will read your journal, do not worry about language or punctuation; simply record your thoughts as they occur to you. It is hard to understand where to start when writing a diary entry, but writing about your everyday activities is a good approach to get your thoughts flowing.

Remember that writing about your ideas, hopes, concerns, frustrations, and any other feelings you are experiencing in your notebook may be a terrific stress reliever, so try to write about them.

A stress journal can help you in identifying your regular stressors and how you deal with them. Keep a notebook or use a stress tracker on your phone to keep track of your stress levels. You will be able to see patterns and common triggers if you keep a daily log. Try to incorporate the following things to help you make sense of your stress:

- What was the source of your stress? (Guess if you are not sure)
- How you physically and emotionally felt?
- How you reacted to the situation?
- What you did to feel better?

Being Aware of Stress Signs

Although it may seem self-evident that you can tell when you are stressed, many of us spend so much time frazzled that we have forgotten what it is like when our nervous systems are in balance: when we are calm but alert and focused. If this describes you, listening to your body can help you detect when you are stressed. Your eyes may feel heavy, and you may lay your head on your hand when you are fatigued. When you are happy, it is easy to laugh. When you are stressed, your body will also let you know. Make it a practice to pay heed to your body's signals.

- Examine your body: Do you have stiff or aching muscles? Do you have a tight, cramped, or painful stomach? Do you have clenched hands or a clenched jaw?

- Pay attention to your breathing: Is it difficult for you to take a deep breath? One hand should be on your stomach, while the other should be on your chest. With each breath, notice how your hands rise and fall. Keep track of when you fully breathe and when you "forget" to breathe.

Finding Response for a Quick Stress Relief

Internally, the "fight-or-flight" stress reaction causes your blood pressure to increase, your heart to beat quicker, and your muscles to constrict. Your immune system is depleted as a result of your body's hard work. People, on the other hand, react to stress in different ways on the outside.

The greatest approach to relieve stress rapidly is to understand your stress response:

- If you are prone to being furious, overly emotional, agitated, or tense when you are stressed, you will benefit from stress-relieving activities that can calm you down.
- If you are prone to being sad, withdrawn, or spaced out when you are stressed, you will benefit from stress-relieving activities that are engaging and energetic.

Do you know about the "frozen" or the immobilization response?

A history of trauma is frequently linked to the immobilization stress response. When confronted with stressful conditions, you may feel completely trapped and powerless to act. Your goal is to reboot your nervous system and reactivate the body's natural "fight-or-flight" stress reaction in order to break free from your "frozen" position. Walking, swimming, sprinting, climbing or tai chi are all examples of physical activities that utilize both your arms and legs. Instead of focusing on your thoughts, concentrate on your body and the feelings you feel in your limbs as you move. This mindfulness component may assist your nervous system is becoming "unstuck" and moving forward.

Use Your Senses

You must first determine which sensory experiences are most beneficial to you. This may necessitate some trial and error. Keep track of how quickly your stress levels decrease as you use different senses. Also, be as accurate as possible. What is the exact sound or movement that has the most impact on you?

Explore a range of sensory experiences so you will always have a stress-relieving tool no matter where you are. The following samples are meant to serve as a starting point. Allow your mind to run wild as you come up with new things to test. You will know when you have found the proper sensory technique.

- Smell

  - Light a scented candle.

  - Take a whiff of roses or another flower.

  - Apply your favorite cologne or perfume.

  - Breathe pure, fresh air outdoors.

- Try different essential oils.

- Sight

    - To spice up your workspace, add a plant or flowers.

    - Take a look at a treasured photo or memento.

    - Enjoy nature's splendor in a garden, on the beach, in a park, or in your own home.

    - Close your eyes and imagine a relaxing and refreshing environment.

    - Colors that uplift your spirits should be all around you.

- Taste

Slowing down and indulging in a favorite treat can be incredibly relaxing, but mindless eating will just add to your waistline and stress. The idea is to enjoy your sense of taste in proportion and with awareness.

    - Take a small piece of dark chocolate and enjoy it.

    - Take a piece of sugarless gum and chew it.

    - Sip a cup of tea or coffee, or a cool beverage

    - Enjoy a crunchy, healthful snack (celery, carrots, or trail mix.)

    - Take a bite out of a perfectly ripe peach.

- Touch

- Pet a cat or a parrot

- Wrap yourself with a blanket to keep warm.

- Keep a reassuring object in your hands (a stuffed animal, a favorite memento).

- Wear clothing that is gentle on the skin.

- Give yourself a hand or neck massage.

• Sound

- Listen to something that is peaceful or uplifting.

- Listen to the sounds of nature: crashing waves, rustling trees, and birds singing.

- Wind chimes can be hung near an open window.

- Purchase a tiny fountain for your home or business to enjoy the relaxing sound of running water.

Vocal toning, as odd as it may sound, is a technique for lowering the stress chemicals adrenaline and cortisol. Before a meeting with your employer, try sneaking away to a quiet spot for a few minutes of toning and watch how much more focused and relaxed you feel. It works by working out the inner ear's small muscles, which help you catch the higher frequencies of human speech that convey emotion and reveal what someone is actually trying to say. You will not only feel more at ease in that encounter, but you will also be able to understand what he is trying to say.

How to do it?

Simply produce "mmmm" sounds with your teeth slightly apart and lips together while sitting up straight. Change the volume and pitch until you feel a pleasant vibration in your face and eventually in your heart and stomach.

If you are having problems figuring out which sensory techniques work best for you, what else can you do?

Look for inspiration anywhere you can, from your daily surroundings to recollections from the past.

- Observe: Observing how others cope with stress might provide you with useful information. Baseball players frequently chew gum before taking the field. Ask your friends how they manage to keep focused under stress.

- Parents: Consider how your parents vented their frustrations. After a long stroll, did your mother feel more relaxed? After a long day at work, did your father work in the yard?

- Memories: Consider how you used to de-stress as a kid. Tactile stimulation could be beneficial if you have a blanket or plush animal. Before an appointment, wear a textured scarf around your neck or bring a piece of soft suede in your pocket.

- Imagination: Try just visualizing vivid sensations when you are stressed. The same relaxing or invigorating impacts on your brain as seeing your baby's photo will occur when you imagine her face. You will never be without a rapid stress alleviation tool if you can imagine a strong sensation.

It's helpful to remember the four A's when deciding between options in any situation:

Stress is a natural nervous system response but some stressors happen at predictable times, e.g., during an office meeting, your commute to work, or family gathering. You can choose handling predicted stressors in two ways: change your response or adjust the issue. When choosing one of the possibilities in any situation, it's helpful to remember the four A's:

1. Avoid Undue Stress

It is unhealthy to avoid managing a hard situation. There are many stressors we can get rid of from our life despite believing otherwise.

• Avoid people who stress you out: Reduce the amount of time you spend with someone who often causes you stress, or cut relations completely.

• Learn to say "no:" Make boundaries and respect them. Be it your professional or personal life, biting more than chewing is a major reason for stress. Know the difference between "musts" and "should" and saying "no" to take on unnecessary work when possible.

• Reduce your to-do list: Observe your obligations, everyday chores, and timetable. Move non-essential jobs to the bottom of the list or erase them entirely if you feel you have too much on your plate.

- Take command of your surroundings: Go for a longer but less-busy route if traffic is stressful for you. Turn off the television if the news makes you nervous. If visit to the grocery store bothers you, shop on the internet.

2. Alter the Situation

If you can't avoid a difficult situation, try to change it. For example, changing the way you interact and function in your daily life.

- Express your emotions instead of hiding them: You should be more assertive and share your concerns in a respectful and open manner if someone or something is troubling you. Say upfront that you only have ten minutes to talk if you need to prepare for an exam and your talkative roommate just got home. If you do not share your emotions, bitterness will grow, and raise your stress levels.

- Make an effort to find a balance between family and employment, social activities and alone time, daily responsibilities and downtime in your schedule. Burnout is caused by all effort and no leisure.

- Be prepared to compromise: If you ask somebody to modify their behavior, show them that you are ready to change your own. It will be more probable that you will reach a happy medium if you are both ready to compromise a little.

3. Adapt to the Stressful Situation

If you can't change the stressor, change yourself. You can respond to unfavorable occurrences and regain control by changing your expectations and attitude.

- Look at the bigger picture: Examine the situation from a different perspective. Will the issue make a difference in a month? Is it worth getting stressed about? If you think the answer is no, you should devote your efforts and time to do something else.

- Reframe problems: While you are in a tough position, look at things in a more positive perspective. Do not be annoyed by a traffic delay but consider it a chance to enjoy some alone time or listen to your favorite radio station.

- Practice gratitude: When you are feeling stressed, take some time to think about all the things you feel grateful for in your life. It can also include your own abilities and characteristics. This simple method can help you in keeping a clear viewpoint on your life.

- Adjust your expectations: Perfectionism is another major stressor that you can leave behind. Stop expecting perfection. Have appropriate expectations for others and yourself, and try to accept some things as "good enough."

4. Accept the Situation

In some instances, stress is unavoidable. Unavoidable stressors include the death of a loved one, the national recession, and significant illness. Accepting things as they are is the most effective way to deal with stress under these circumstances. Acceptance is difficult, but it is less difficult in the long run than battling a situation you can't change.

- Look for the silver lining: When faced with significant challenges, try to perceive them as opportunities for personal growth. If your poor judgments led to a stressful situation, reflect on them and learn from them.

- Do not try to control what you cannot control: Many things in life are beyond our control, especially other people's actions. Instead of worrying about them, concentrate on the things you can control, such as how you respond to challenges.

- Feel free to express yourself: Even if there is nothing you can do to change the unpleasant circumstances, expressing what you are going through can be quite relieving. Make an appointment with a therapist or talk to a trusted friend.

- Learn to forgive: Recognize that we live in an imperfect world where people make mistakes. Let go of your resentments and wrath. You may release yourself from negative energy by forgiving and moving on.

Making Time for Fun and Relaxation

By scheduling "me" time, taking charge, and maintaining a positive outlook, you may lessen stress in your life. Do not get stuck in the hustle and bustle of life to the point where you forget to look after yourself. Self-care is a requirement, not a luxury. If you arrange time for enjoyment and relaxation on a regular basis, you will be better able to handle life's stresses.

- Make "Me" time: Incorporate rest and relaxation into your daily routine. Allow no other obligations to get in the way. This is your opportunity to detach from all responsibilities and re-energize.

- Do something you enjoy every day. Make time for your favorite hobbies, such as astronomy, tennis, or cycling.

- Maintain your sense of humor: Laughter aids your body's stress-reduction efforts in a variety of ways.

- Start a relaxing routine: Relaxation methods such as yoga, meditation, and deep breathing activate the body's relaxation response, which is the opposite of the fight or flight or mobilization stress response. As you learn and apply these strategies, your stress levels will decrease, and your mind and body will become calm and centered.

Learning to Connect with Others

It's quite relaxing to spend time with someone who knows you and makes you feel safe. In reality, face-to-face interaction triggers a hormonal cascade that counteracts the body's defensive "fight-or-flight" response. It is a natural stress reliever from nature. So, make it a point to contact family and friends on a regular basis—and in person.

Remember that the individuals you talk to, do not have to be able to help you deal with your stress. Simply put, they must be good listeners. Also, don't let concerns about appearing weak or burdensome prevent you from speaking up. Those who care about you will appreciate your trust. It will only serve to strengthen your bond.

Of course, having a close buddy to lean on when you are stressed is not always practical, but you can strengthen your resistance to life's stresses by cultivating and maintaining a network of close friends.

Making Quick Stress Relief a Habit

Midst of crisis, it is difficult to remember to use your senses. It will feel simpler at first to just give in to the pressure and stiffen up. However, using your senses will become second nature over time. Consider how you would learn to drive or play golf. It takes more than one instruction to master a skill; you must practice until it becomes second nature. Though you do not tune in to your body during difficult circumstances, you will eventually feel as if you forget something. Here is how to turn it into a habit:

• Identify and target: Consider one low-level stressor, such as commuting, that you know will occur multiple times each week. Make a promise to yourself to always attack that stressor with immediate stress reduction. Target a second stressor after a few weeks, and so on.

• Begin small: Start with a predicted low-level source of stress, such as making sitting down to pay bills or dinner at the end of a long day, instead of testing your rapid stress relief techniques on a high-level source of stress.

- Enjoy the process: If something is not working, do not push it. Continue until you have discovered what works best for you. It should be enjoyable as well as notably relaxing.

- Experiment with sensory input: Bring a scented handkerchief one day, chocolate the next, and movement the third day if you are practicing rapid stress alleviation on your commute to work. Experiment until you come up with a clear winner.

- Talk about it. Informing friends or family members about the stress-relieving techniques you are experimenting with will assist you in incorporating them into your daily routine. As an extra benefit, it will almost certainly spark a lively discussion: everyone can relate to the subject of stress.

Managing Your Time Better

Poor time management can worsen anxiety. When you're overworked and behind schedule, it's difficult to stay cool and focused. Plus, you will be tempted to avoid or reduce all of the good activities you should be doing to manage stress, such as socializing and getting adequate sleep. There are various methods for you to improve your work-life balance.

- Check to see whether you're taking on more than you're capable of: Try not to schedule events in a row or cram too much into a single day. We have a propensity to underestimate the time required to complete an activity.

• Make a to-do list: Make a list of what you need to get done and prioritize it. Prioritize the tasks with the highest priority first. If you have something particularly unpleasant or stressful to do, get it done as quickly as possible. As a result, you'll have a better time the remainder of the day.

• Break down tasks into manageable chunks: Make a step-by-step strategy if a major undertaking becomes daunting. Focus on one realistic task at a time rather than trying to do everything at once.

• Assign responsibilities to others: You do not have to do everything yourself at home, school, or at work. If others are capable of performing the task, why not delegate it to them? Allow yourself to let go of the need to control or supervise every aspect. In the process, you will be releasing unnecessary stress.

Making Exercise a Habit

When you're anxious, the last thing you want to do is exercise. However, physical activity is a terrific stress reliever, and you don't have to spend hours at the gym or be an athlete to get the benefits. Exercising releases endorphins, which make you feel good, and it can also be a great way to forget about your problems. People who exercise regularly are improbable to suffer from anxiety than those who do not. There are several causes for this:

- Exercise reduces stress hormones in your body, such as cortisol, in the long run. It aids in releasing endorphins, which are feel-good chemicals that also work as natural painkillers.

- Exercise can help you have a better night's sleep, which can be impaired by anxiety and stress.

- Regular exercise can help you feel confident in your body and competent, which can help you feel better mentally.

While you will gain the most benefit from a minimum 30-minute-long exercise on a regular basis, it is fine to progressively increase your fitness level. Small acts of kindness can build up to a lot of positive energy. All you have to do now is get up and get started. Here are a few simple methods to add fitness into your everyday schedule:

- Take a walk with your dog.

- To get to the store, walk or ride your bike.

- Park the car at the end of the parking lot and walk the rest of the distance.

- Use the stairs instead of the elevator at home or at work.

- Play an activity-based video game or Ping-Pong etc., with your children.

- As you work out, pair up with an exercise buddy and cheer each other on.

While any type of physical activity can assist relieve stress and tension, rhythmic activities are particularly beneficial. Walking, swimming, running, tai chi, cycling, and aerobics are all good options. But whatever you do, make sure you enjoy it so you will be more inclined to remain with it.

Make an effort and pay attention to your body and the physical (and occasionally emotional) sensations you feel as you move while exercising. Consider how the sunlight or air feels on your skin or how you can coordinate your breathing with your motions. Including this mindfulness, the component will help you break out from the negative mental cycle that often comes with overwhelming stress.

Changing Your Lifestyle

Some other healthy lifestyle choices coupled with regular exercise can help you become more resistant to stress.

• Maintain a balanced diet: Be attentive to what you consume because well-nourished bodies are better at coping with stress. To keep your mind fresh and your energy up, start your day off well with breakfast and eat good, balanced meals throughout the day.

A bad diet can make you more receptive to stress. Emotional eating and grabbing for high-sugar, high-fat foods may bring a short-term sensation of relief, but they will only add to your long-term stress. Potato chips and cookies, for example, can trigger a blood sugar increase. When your blood sugar levels drop, you may feel more stressed and anxious. A balanced diet might help you deal with stress in the long run. Mood management and energy balance are aided by foods like avocado, eggs, and walnuts.

- Avoid sugar and caffeine: Caffeine and sugar give short "highs" that are frequently followed by a slump in energy and mood. You will feel more relaxed and sleep better if you reduce your intake of soft drinks, chocolate, coffee, and sugary snacks.

- Avoid cigarettes and narcotics: Self-medicating with cigarettes or narcotics may provide a quick fix for stress, but the relief is fleeting. Deal with difficulties directly on and with a clear mind, rather than avoiding or masking them.

- Make sure you get enough rest: A good night's sleep is beneficial to both your mind and body. If you are tired, you will be more stressed because it may cause you to think irrationally. In studies, even partial sleep deprivation has been shown to have a significant impact on mood. Participants who were only permitted 4.5 hours of sleep every night for a week felt more concerned, enraged, unhappy, and mentally exhausted, according to University of Pennsylvania researchers. The individuals' moods improved dramatically once they resumed normal sleep.

These ten steps can help you minimize and handle stress, so it does not interfere with living your best life.

Chapter 9:

How to Overcome and Reduce Stress and Anxiety?

This is a short chapter, but one of the most important ones in the book. We'll look at some of the stress-relieving options available to you. These are time tested and proven techniques that can help you let off a little bit of steam or prevent it from even building up.

Exercise

One of the best things you can do is take up a regular exercise routine. For many people, the first thing they do when someone suggests that they get more exercise is protest that they don't have enough time to work out.

You literally only have to dedicate one hour of your day to exercise to get real benefits. Go for a run, a brisk stroll, some light weight lifting, or join a gym if you really want to take it to the next level.

Whatever you do, set a goal of spending one hour of your day on physical activity, no matter what. You don't have to do the same thing every day, as long as you do something.

Remove yourself from the source of your anxiety.

This may come off as a little bit harsh, but even if it's your family that's stressing you out, you have to get away from them for a little bit. The same applies to situations where work is the cause of your stress or in any other instance where there is a particular situation or person that's bothering you.

You'll find that, when you go back to dealing with the situation, you'll be quite a bit more patient and far less likely to explode.

Reassess Your Attitude, Realistically

Take stock of your attitude and consider how it might be contributing to your feeling stressed in certain situations. Be open-minded to the idea that your attitude may be entirely justified.

For example, if you feel like you can never get ahead, no matter how much you work, maybe your job really doesn't pay you enough. Perhaps it's time to ask for a raise or look for a new position. Accepting that may entail stress just as much as the existing situation does, but at least it's stress for which there is a clear resolution.

Cut Out the Caffeine

This is something that most hard-working people never want to hear. Truth be told, caffeine raises your tension levels by increasing the amount of stress hormones in your bloodstream, stimulating your central nervous system and interfering with your sleep patterns.

A little bit of caffeine is acknowledged to actually be helpful in some situations. It helps you concentrate; it wakes you up rather quickly in the morning and, somewhat counterintuitively, it can actually be relaxing to have a cup of coffee.

If you're overdoing it, however, be sure to reassess whether or not you need to be drinking as much coffee, tea or any other caffeinated beverages as you do during the day. If you can cut back, it will generally help you quite a bit with reducing your overall stress levels.

Pay Attention to How Well You Sleep

Being under a lot of stress is almost guaranteed to interfere with your sleep patterns. Harboring all of that anxiety and, sometimes, anger can make it difficult to get to sleep at all. When you do get to sleep, it's not likely that you're going to sleep soundly.

One of the best ways to bust stress is to take a look at your sleep patterns and, if they're becoming erratic, work on ways to regulate them. Every day, make an attempt to go to bed and wake up at the same time. This establishes a habit of falling asleep and obtaining as much rest as possible, making it more likely that you will wake up refreshed rather than resentful of another night of poor sleep.

Cutting down on caffeine plays into this. Ideally, stop drinking caffeine in the early afternoon so that it isn't keeping you awake later at night. It can take hours for caffeine to process through your system.

Establish Boundaries

Establishing boundaries is a great way to keep your stress levels reduced. All it entails is telling people what you need from them and letting them know when they've crossed a line with you.

This applies to everyone. Put your boss on notice if he or she yells at you or otherwise bullies you. Tell them their actions are unacceptable and that if they continue, you will retire. Sometimes even the people in charge need to be put in their place.

In personal relationships, if somebody's doing something that makes you feel anxiety, tell them about it. You don't necessarily have to be firm, as you would if somebody was being aggressive toward you, but let them know that it causes you stress. Sometimes, they may not even know that they were causing a problem for you and will be more than happy to change their behavior a bit so they no longer are contributing to your anxiety levels.

Journal Your Days

Keep at least a very simple journal of your days. The idea here is to write down the things that stick out in your mind and, in particular, to record those things that caused you to feel stressed. This is one of the most effective ways to identify what's really bothering you and where you may need to look at making a change in your life.

If you're not a good writer, don't be put off by the idea of journaling. Nobody sees the journal but you, and it doesn't have to be written in proper English. If you tend to write in bulleted lists or are one of those people who keep notes by drawing pictures, go ahead and do that. All you have to do now is scribble something down to help you remember what's been upsetting you. By going back and reviewing it later, you can start to see patterns that may indicate situations that aren't working for you and that seem to be persistent parts of your life.

Any one of these techniques can go a long way toward reducing the levels of stress that you experience on a day-to-day basis. If you can't incorporate all of them into your life, at least try to add one of them. For example, if you hate keeping a journal, go ahead and start running to let off a little bit of steam.

Remember that everything you do to cope with your stress, even if it turns out that the method, you're trying isn't effective, is one step toward finding a successful solution. You'll start to notice benefits if you continue with it.

Chapter 10:

Destress Your Mind and Soul

Control Your Thoughts

Giving up control

Stress management is a very complex phenomenon. Something must be controlled to govern it, for example, testing your shower for the amount of hot water. You activate the water and adjust the hot and cold-water mixture to regulate the temperature. If it's wrong, you walk into the shower and start lathering. Sadly, at your discretion, you do not have "warm" or "cold" pressure faucets. You cannot merely turn positive thoughts and emotions while at the same time, turning off disturbing and painful feelings.

Managing means understanding that all the factors involved in any situation cannot be controlled and governed. You know that when you handle something, you cannot manage or operate around all of the variables involved. You live together with a lack of control and continue to advance towards your target.

While your mind can be of great help in managing potential external stressors, it can lead to stress when coping with potential internal stressors. Note, the brain is a 24/7 non-stop machine of thinking and feeling. That's what he thinks and feels. It is always on, and all the processing of it cannot be controlled or eliminated. Trying to stop the thoughts and feelings is like trying to stop a disappearing train. The best thing you can do sometimes is slow it down and focus on one or two words.

Studies show that it is getting worse to try to control, stop, or remove disturbing thoughts, own script, visual images, and unpleasant emotions. By concentrating your full attention and trying to control disturbing thoughts or uncomfortable feelings, it intensifies your strength of mind.

You can even demonstrate this by thinking of a genuinely fun picture, not stressful like a bright red, white, and a blue beach ball. Think of how you feel when the ball is thrown up and caught as it drifts quickly back to you. Close your eyes and think about that luminous beach ball you throw up and down thoroughly. Think of it for a few seconds. Stop thinking about it now. I want you to work hard to stop worrying about the beach ball, which is bright red, white, and blue. Come on, try to stop thinking about the beach ball very, really hard. Continue to read this section and stop thinking about the beach ball. What happens when you try to control the beach ball? Are they gone or intensified? In most situations, it did not make them go away when trying to control your thoughts.

A key element of replenishing your pressure is to learn how to shift your focus from disturbing thoughts, private texts, traumatic mental images, emotions, and actions that fit your beliefs. This means being more prepared to participate in helpful behaviors and to create better environments. Control and willingness are inverses; the more distressing thoughts and unpleasant feelings you try to control, the less willing you are to take action. Inverse, the more able you are to accept troublesome thoughts and unpleasant emotions, the less need you have to control them to act.

Control and the willingness to take values-related actions are the key ingredients of rethinking as a defense against stress while it coexists with pain and suffering. You often get trapped and do nothing when you are unwilling to take action because you need to control all of the variables involved in potentially stressful situations.

Dealing with Pain

Pain is quite literally a painful topic to deal with, and we have powerful inbuilt mechanisms to deal with it. There are two types of pain that you need to be aware of. The first is acute pain, which cannot be cured through mindfulness. This is the pain that results from a physical injury or a problem that has occurred in your life. The pain of this kind needs a medical solution and not a spiritual one.

The second kind of pain is chronic pain. The origin of chronic pain may be physical, but there is a huge emotional and cognitive component to it which mindfulness can address. While the elimination of pain is a stretch, reducing the burden, you carry as a result of it is certainly possible. Research shows that meditation and other mindfulness practices can help address chronic pain (Penman, 2019).

While meditation by itself is very effective, applying an entire framework of mindfulness to the issue is a better approach. So, how do you do this? Well, the first step is to begin by investigating the pain.

Step One

The common reaction we have to pain is to clench our muscles around the area that causes pain and then deeply wish it goes away. In short, our reaction has both a physical and emotional component to it, and in the throes of pain, it is difficult to separate the two. Mindfulness will allow you to do just that.

Why is it important to separate the two parts of your reaction? Well, for one thing, your emotions to the pain often make it far worse than it really is. Think of a child who falls to the ground when she thinks no one is watching. More often than not, the child will dust themselves off and keep running. However, when the child senses her parents are watching, and as she sees the looks of concern as they rush towards her, she will inevitably start crying.

In this case, the negative emotions of the parents lead the child to believe her pain is far worse than it actually is. Most of the pain is just plain emotional exaggeration, though. A similar thing happens to us as adults as well, even if we don't shed tears. This heightened emotion causes us to react physically to the pain in inappropriate ways as well.

While clenching muscles around the painful area is a normal reaction, you'll find when performing your body scan practice that the extent of this clenching goes far beyond just the affected area. Clenching your muscles to this extent communicates a stress response to your brain, and it accordingly executes what it needs to.

A stress response is your body's mechanism of dealing with mortal threats. When your brain detects a mortal threat, it redirects blood flow to your limbs, prioritizes certain bodily functions, such as physical movement and respiration, to enable a quick flight and deprioritizes others, such as digestion. All of this puts tremendous stress on your body. Adrenaline is secreted, which gives you an additional boost and makes you temporarily immune to pain.

This state of affairs cannot last for long because it puts a huge load on your internal organs and functions. If you spend too much time in such situations, your brain will simply shut down and demand rest. Prolonged exposure will result in traumas like PTSD and so on. While the stress you feel might not be of the same degree as a mortal threat, its very presence puts a strain on your body.

This is why by relaxing your body, you can remove the stressful interpretation of events your brain is currently stuck processing. Another way mindfulness recommends is to ride the pain and notice how it ebbs and flows.

Step Two

Should you suffer when you feel pain? Think about that question a little bit more before thinking of an answer. You see, pain and suffering are two different things. Pain is what the stimulus is. Suffering is born out of your reaction to the pain. So, with this in mind, ask yourself, is it necessary to suffer when you feel pain?

The simple answer is no; it isn't. In reality, though, it is difficult to live this way. We're used to blending our suffering together with our experience of pain so that it forms one seamless reaction. Mindfulness will teach you to separate the two. The first thing to examine is whether you have any resistance to allowing your emotions to flow.

We're taught a lot of things about exhibiting our emotions, ranging from presenting a stoic outlook towards things to flat out denying the validity of the ones we feel. The general wisdom is to acknowledge emotions and let them be. This is, unfortunately, not enough.

The acknowledgment must be accompanied by acceptance if it is to be useful. Mere acknowledgment is simply recognizing that emotions exist but doesn't imply engagement with them. Similarly, to let your emotions be is to give them some space to exist but not engage with them anymore.

You need to accept and let your emotions pass through you. The key to doing this is to understand your choice with regard to responding to those emotions. By observing and striving to maintain equanimity, you improve your ability to deal with pain and detach the emotional response from the stimulus. Hence, you will be free to feel the pain, but you need not compound your suffering by reacting inappropriately to it.

Step Three

The third and most important step is to set your intention to live in the present moment. Deal only with what is making itself known to you right now, and don't worry about what it means for the future. If you're experiencing pain at this moment, then deal with it now. If it presents itself in the next moment, deal with it then.

As an example, if you bump your head on something pretty badly, experience the pain, and feel the negative emotion welling up inside you. It hurts, and your emotions are valid. Don't bottle them up. Try to separate the physical sensation from your emotional reaction, but if you can't do this, don't worry about it.

You might be worried if you're bleeding. Well, check to see if you are. Worrying about whether you're bleeding and then thinking you will need to go to the hospital and get yourself checked out and then worrying about how much money that's going to cost you and the amount of time you'll need to spend doing this is simply compounding your suffering.

It is also traveling into the future to see what might happen. Mindfulness requires you to stay in the present and see what happens. Feel your pain and let your emotions through. Once that's done, get back to what you were doing and be on your way. As long as the pain expresses itself, feel it, and learn to love it. This is a part of living after all, and you cannot have pleasure without pain. So, accept it and allow it to move through you.

Suggestions To Reduce Negative Mind-Sets

1.   Do not overthink

There's not anything more manic and more unwanted than over-thinking. Whenever you over-think, the human mind is too cluttered to be in its finest. Your motives differ, and at the close of your afternoon, you might continue to be unsure exactly what your priorities will be. That is quite typical with the sort of mindset.

Certainly, one of the greatest ways never to overthink will always be to take a while for you to meditate. Even 20 minutes of meditation every day will decelerate your negative thinking patterns and also allow you to concentrate on what's important. Check it out for quite a couple of weeks and then see the change in your over-thinking patterns.

2.   Watch chances, not issues

Writers are a really sensitive team of an individual. We have a tendency to be quite negative, and also, we concentrate on the issues and feel trapped with these. And that may set us up for perceiving and translating everything. Whatever things occur to people every single day, from rejections to not being in a position to finish our everyday word counts, we translate each one these matters into negative provisions.

But once we shift our thinking patterns from negative into optimistic ones and view every problem as a chance for learning, our cognitive performance enhances, and we have a tendency to be considered a whole lot more productive and fulfilled. There are courses embedded in every one of these issues. What we all want to do would behave the opportunity to ascertain exactly what they've been.

3. *Confront negative ideas mind on*

Sometimes we are our own worst enemies. We can concentrate on our negative thoughts by what we're doing. This may make patterns of negative thinking that may persist for quite a while if we aren't attentive. Ergo, it's crucial for authors to prevent destructive thoughts in their own tracks. Remember, you are simply a brand-new blossom, and you are attempting to handle an extremely hard atmosphere. You certainly can perform it; however, it's going to be quite tough to accomplish so in the beginning.

By following this advice, you'll undoubtedly be taking very good measures to prevent adverse thoughts and mindsets. This will enhance your imagination and general productivity. And also, this can be a win-win for most authors and outside.

Manage Your Emotions

How to Identify Emotions

Emotions refer to the way you react to a situation. It is not an easy task doing so; it takes time and patience. Different people have different emotions, and you need to take time for you to identify the right emotion.

So, why should you even identify the emotions in the first place? Emotions come in three parts – the subjective, physiological, and expressive component. The subjective component refers to how you experience emotion, while the physiological component refers to how the body reacts to the emotion while the expressive component refers to how you behave when you respond to the emotion.

These elements play a big role in how you respond to emotion.

The roles that emotions play in our lives

They motivate us to take action

The emotions dictate the way you react to the situation. For instance, when you are faced with an exam, you will feel anxious about how well you will perform and how the test will affect the results you get. Because of the responses, you might be forced to study better. The emotion allows you to take some action and improves the outcome.

Emotions also allow us to decide which actions to take; usually, the actions are aimed at helping us to experience more positive emotions while we reduce the probability of negative emotions.

Emotions Help Us Survive

Emotions are a way for us to avoid danger, survive ad reproduce. When we get angry, the next natural reaction is to confront what is causing the irritation. When we are afraid, we will most likely run.

Emotions play the role of motivating us to take action quickly, something that will increase the chances of success and survival.

They Help Us Make Decisions

Emotions have the ability to influence the decisions that we make. For instance, when we get annoyed, we look for a way to change the situation. Even when we have situations that require us to decide purely by rationality and logic, we still work by emotions.

Emotions Help Us Communicate

When we communicate with other people, it is vital that we give them clues that will make them understand our situation better. These clues involve emotions that we then display through body language. This can be in the form of facial expressions that are connected to certain emotions that we experience.

In some cases, it can involve us stating how we feel directly. For instance, when we tell someone that we are sad, happy, or frightened, then we ate, giving them vital information that they can utilize to take action.

They Help Us to Understand Others

Just the way we give other people an idea of how we feel when we show them the emotions we go through; the emotions of other people also give us an idea of what other people are thinking or planning.

When we know how to identify and interpret emotions, we have the capacity to react to their emotions the right way. When we learn about emotions, we get to react the right way to them, which means more meaningful relationships with other people.

How to Recognize Emotions

For you to manage your emotions, you first need to learn how to identify them the right way. A significant percentage of people try to ignore emotional reactions, letting the emotions build up within them. When this happens, the result is impaired ability to use their emotions in a productive way.

Other people recognize the emotions but find it difficult to control them, and they find themselves at the mercy of the emotions.

For you to use your emotions the right way, you need first to identify the emotions the right way. Let us look at the best way to identify the emotions:

1. *Understand the Trigger*

The first step towards identifying the emotion is first to know what caused it. This will help you to describe the events that led to an emotional event. In this step, try to stick to facts alone.

You can write down the event that led to the emotion so that you have it clear in your mind.

2. *Why Do You Think It Happened?*

The next step is to identify the possible causes that led to an emotional event. This is crucial because it determines the meaning that you give to the situation that happened. The type of emotional event that led to the issue will determine the way you react to the event in question.

3. *How the Situation Made You Feel*

The next step is to determine how the emotional event made you feel both physically and emotionally. This will help you see whether the emotion resulted in a positive or negative reaction.

You need to notice both the positive as well as the negative emotional and physical reactions that you felt when it happened. Notice any physical feelings that you experience, such as tightness in the body.

4. *What Was Your Reaction*

You need to ask yourself this question so that you understand your urges. However, for the process to be effective, you need to make sure you are completely honest. It might be painful to admit some of the urges that you felt when the event happened. When we face some situations, we, at times, get strange urges to react differently. Some of the emotions that we go through might make us regret later on.

You need to compare your reaction at the moment that things happened and how you usually react normally. This will tell you whether you managed to control the urge or you failed to do so.

5. *What Did You Do and Speak?*

The next step would be to understand what you actually said or did due to the emotions. Even though you didn't manage to respond the right way, you need to be honest with yourself about how you handled the situation. You also need to understand how the decision you made impacted on the situation. This can be a good learning experience for you.

Once you evaluate your reaction, you can then use the situation to learn how to handle another situation that might arise.

6. *How Did the Reaction Affect You Later on?*

The final step in identifying the emotions is to understand the consequences of the actions that you took. If you said some words during the event, how did they affect you? On the other hand, if you acted in a certain way, how did it affect you later on?

So, if you find yourself being overly attached to your emotions next time, you need to ask yourself what happened and take the time to observe how you react when it happens. Go through these steps so that you can recognize your emotions. Once you practice and get used to these steps, you will be able to identify your emotions the right way and then choose the best way to respond to situations.

Avoid Perfectionism in Emotions

There is no such thing as perfect in this world and even less so when it comes to emotions. A person who seeks perfectionism in emotions thinks that they should always be in a positive emotional state. This line of thought is living in denial of the setbacks that occur in life. Experiencing negative emotions is equally as natural as feeling positive ones, and a person cannot choose to experience one feeling while denying another permanently.

People who try to practice emotional perfectionism are the type to tell others who are experiencing negative emotions to think positively. In doing so, they undermine both the adverse event and the feelings of the party concerned because negative emotions cannot just magically cease to exist. These people think that they can control emotions so entirely that they can prevent themselves from experiencing the negative ones. They also believe that they are capable of capturing and maintaining positive ones.

This scenario illustrates how seeking perfectionism in emotions can distort someone's reality and give them a false sense of control. They have an illusion of command where they believe that they are only ever in a positive mindset. However, the reality is that perfectionism makes their emotional experience worse. It becomes a case where one denies a particular negative emotion so much that they end up experiencing that same emotion when the denial does not work. It results in situations where an individual goes through a lot of stress about or becomes angry about being angry.

There is a saying that if a person wants to heal, they should let themselves fall ill. Similarly, if one wants to handle negative emotions, one should first accept them. One should avoid seeking perfection in feelings because the essence of perfectionism is to deny the existence and experience of negative emotions.

Compassion for Self

Negative emotions arise from adverse events that happen to someone. Therefore, a person should learn to love himself or herself and to show kindness to self. The external situation is already terrible and unkind to them, so there is no need for someone to be mean to himself or herself. Such an action only adds fuel to the fire and can make one feel worse than they already do and even lose themselves in the resulting negative emotions.

People sometimes say, "No one loves me more than me." If that is true, how do people find themselves being kind, supportive, and compassionate to others but not to themselves? They will hug a friend who lost their job and encourage a student who did not perform well in an examination. However, the same people will also find themselves wallowing in feelings of failure after having an unsuccessful interview for a job. They may start to call themselves fools for even having enough faith to try the evaluation in the first place.

Having self-compassion is being able to accept the adverse events and results that take place in life as well as being able to soothe and encourage oneself under challenging circumstances. It recognizes that life is full of up and downs, and experiencing the negatives and failures does not define who one is. Compassion for self enables one to go through collapse or defeat successfully while simultaneously learning from the experience. It helps a person to better prepare for future trials and encourages them to continue trying despite a lack of success in the past.

Unfortunate things or events will always take place in people's lives. They should learn to comfort and encourage themselves as they experience the accompanying negative emotions. This compassion for self helps them to manage and control their negative feelings, which results in better care of one's emotional and mental state.

Meditation

This practice aims to achieve mental clarity and calm emotions. One achieves these by training their thoughts in terms of awareness and attention. Meditation enables one to observe their feelings and thoughts without judgment to understand them. The resulting comprehension makes a person able to manage his or her emotions effectively, especially negative sentiments.

Meditation and mindfulness relate closely but differ in that mindfulness is the ability to engage in the present moment fully while meditation is one of the skills that enable mindfulness. Thus, a person should learn this skill to gain access to more ways of handling negative emotions. One learns how to focus and control specific physical actions like breathing techniques, which they can then apply when trying to manage negative emotions and the effects they have. The skill is especially useful in dealing with intense negative feelings like rage, which can quickly spiral out of control and cause more damage.

Meditation allows one to have better control of their emotions, which in turn will help them to deal with the problem or situation in a constructive way. The focus on calm and awareness helps a person to handle negative emotions in a composed and meaningful way.

Chapter 11:

Social, Spiritual, and Environmental, Strategies for Stress Relief

People exist in social, natural, and spiritual environments, and it might be surprising that changing the environment, as opposed to changing oneself, can bring about a transformative change in helping to relieve stress.

There are other simple ways to get relieved from stress, aside from deliberately manipulating the body and mind. So far, we've discussed different psychological, physical, and biological techniques for getting relieved from stress. Now we will talk about how you can relieve stress by altering your surroundings.

Sensory Immersion

The artificial urgency of working and family life, meetings, deadlines, goals, unpleasant chores, etc., temporarily goes away when you deepen yourself in certain sensations, and the elusive solution to the actual meaning of existence feels closer at such times.

One of the best methods to transform one's relationship with life, and get transformed by the environment, is to deepen oneself in a natural sensory experience. This can mean being deliberate and taking out time to appreciate nature. Go for a hike in the mountains, a swim in the lake or ocean, cross country ski in the fool-hills, have a picnic by the creek in the woods, go camping.

Find a way to escape from civilization.

Notice the scents, textures, shapes, colors, and taste in your environment. When encountered with a riot of colors in a wild landscape, it makes gaining a sense of awe easier, and even for something greater in yourself. It doesn't have to be pure wilderness either. Take in the roar of the ocean, the taste of home-made food, the smell of flowers in the garden, the soft sensation of kisses.

Judgments and demanding thought patterns are a part of what makes people stressed out. The work of sensory immersion reduces stress for a few various reasons. At the foundational level, it performs as a distraction and a silent interruption to the regular, judgmental, and demanding chatter that forms most people's thoughts. Bypassing this with a direct sensory experience can aid the mind for a period or two, and in the process, temporarily bypass the inner demands that the mind's chatter creates and enforces.

Deliberate sensory immersion will also help to produce dopamine, the hormone that gives a positive, happy sensation capable of reducing the numerous painful and anxiety-induced sensations that are common to a stressed person's life. On another level, individuals can push the balance of their lives in the way of joy by exposing themselves to experiences that can make them feel content and happy.

People don't know the amount of pressure they bring upon themselves until they get a break and realize how crazy and hectic it is to live in such a way. Allowing yourself to have a good break from routine demand, sensory immersion can aid individuals in finding the mental space that is necessary to examine the values that are currently ruling their lives and decide if they need adjustment and changes in order to allow for a more humane and calmer lifestyle. As everyone can derive benefit from non-verbal respite, sensory immersion can bring about additional advantages.

The feeling of awe that comes from allowing yourself to feel and take in the sensations of nature helps individuals become present in the current moment of their life, instead of bothering about the past or future. These experiences can assist in clarifying your motivations and values. When people get in touch with their values, their perception and perspective broaden, and it becomes very easy for them to take control and manage their stress.

The idea of seeking joyful sensations for the sake of joy may sound irresponsible and hedonistic to some. For such critics, it can be suggested that "all work and no play make jack a dull boy." It's not healthy to become hedonists and completely ignore the tasks of life, but it is healthy to regain balance and release the stifling overabundance of responsibility and duty.

It might interest you to note that some of the sensations you loved as a child are still available for you to re-experience, as well as many others.

If I may ask, can you remember the last time you caught snowflakes on your tongue, or picked up a very old-fashioned snowball fight? Or licked the inside of your ice cream bowl? Or maybe listen to the purr of a kitten? There are numerous easy ways to include some sensory joy in your life; you will have a few thoughts on how to do this in a better, if not the best, way for you. There are numerous lists of experiences and sensations that once created joy for you, write down the new ideas as they come. You can then start making frequent appointments to have a re-experience of these memories and some of the great feelings and sensations they produce.

Reducing Stress with Tai Chi, Yoga, and Pilates

Tai Chi

Just like hatha, tai chi entails the constant practice of different postures. This stress relief technique was developed originally in China as a martial-art style used for self-defense. Over the years, it has gradually been used more and more to exercise and facilitate personal development. Tai chi helps to relax the mind and heart. According to research, those that frequently practice enjoy reduced blood pressure as much as those practicing strenuous forms of aerobic exercise.

Movement is continuous and is used to relax and realign the body. A form is a full set of tai chi exercises. There are 37 basic short forms of moves. Like yoga and Pilates, tai chi classes can also be taken at community centers, gyms, or martial art studios. Another effective way of practice is to find videos that teach tai chi moves in the comfort of your house.

Pilates

All of the Pilate's routines are very low impact and work the deep core muscles. Pilates makes the abdomen flat and the back stronger while improving balance and posture, as well as decreasing stress levels. During the early 1990s, Pilates was developed by Joseph Pilates. It can involve using a mat with no other equipment. The mat can work with different resistance apparatus, machine-assisted exercise, or a combination of these methods. This practice is physically demanding and strengthens the body's powerhouse with movements that are performed in a precise manner, along with specialized techniques of breathing and intense mental concentration.

Yoga

There are many types of Yoga. Yoga is divided into Raja Yoga and Hatha Yoga. Hatha yoga is what is popular in the Western Hemisphere, involving complex poses and stretches called asanas. Raja yoga involves the joining of the mind, body, and spirit.

Here we will talk about hatha yoga. In the West, the practice of hatha yoga has been influenced by different teachers who have established different schools, that is, different versions of Yoga to which many people are involved.

One is Iyengar Yoga. This variety of hatha yoga was developed by B.K.S. Iyengar focuses on the slow, proper, and safe performance of different postures.

Another version is Bikram yoga. This has its roots in the work of Bikram Choudhury. It is usually practiced in a room with a hot temperature. It can be strenuous and include sticking to a certain set of postures during every session.

Yet another form of yoga is Ashtanga, which is an associated and also very strenuous yoga form, and also sports yoga, which provides a combined approach based on hatha yoga and some elements from western stretching, Pilate's exercise, and martial arts warm-ups.

Yoga originated in India some thousand years back, and it is one of the ancient techniques used for improving the body and mind. Asanas help to increase strength, balance, and flexibility. Practicing yoga allows the muscles' tension to be relieved, lowers blood pressure, and reduces cholesterol levels. It is one of the most effective and excellent practices of stress relief.

It is very essential that you choose a form of yoga that best suits your personality. If you take a class with an aggressive or fast-paced style when a more precise and slow style suits you, you can do more damage than good.

The Iyengar version of yoga is most likely to give these pros. Over the time of practice, you will gradually become flexible and be able to do increasingly advanced asanas. When you continue practicing yoga, these benefits will come to fruition. But there is a limit to the number of postures you can effectively master.

As with any other new thing you intend on doing, it is important that you are patient with yourself when you begin to study yoga. You can adopt the use of props, like foam bricks and straps, which are recommended for less flexible beginners.

You can try several types of yoga and facilitators to discover the practice and coaching style that suits your abilities and needs. Yoga classes can be taken at health clubs, yoga studios, community centers, and so on. Watching videos or buying books to use at home is another option.

Stress Inoculation Therapy

The term inoculation in SIT has its foundation on the idea that a therapist is inoculating or preparing a patient to be resistant to the threatening effects of stressors in a way similar to how a vaccine will work to make patients resistant to the effect of particular diseases. SIT, Stress Inoculation Therapy is a psychotherapy method that is used to help patients and prepare them in advance to handle events that are stressful, successfully, with no or minimum upset.

At the end of the stress inoculation trials, patients are expected to feel like they can expect pitfalls that may happen during an occasion and also have a workable and practical plan handy to help them avoid those pitfalls. Relapse Prevention Method and Stress Inoculation are conceptually similar. The Relapse Prevention method is used as an additional therapy. Patients are educated about stressful situations, the negative outcome they may be exposed to, knowing when confronted with stress, and the nature at which stress functions in SIT.

There are three phases to Stress Inoculation.

SIT has been done to couples, individuals, and groups, both large and small, from different cultures and backgrounds. The duration of the intervention can be as short as 20 minutes and as long as 41 hours weekly and biweekly sessions. In most cases, there are 8 to 15 sessions of SIT, plus booster and follow-up sessions, which are conducted over a 3-to-12-month period.

In the initial conceptualize phase, the therapist educates the patient about the general nature of stress as well as explaining the essential concepts. For instance, the appraisal and cognitive distortion that is responsible in forming stress reactions. The concept that people always and quite inadvertently make their stress worse by the subconscious operation of poor coping habits will also be communicated. Lastly, the therapist is saddled with developing a clear understanding of the complexity of the stressors the patient is facing.

Instead of the mere obstacles, a very important part of what is communicated in the SIT conceptualization stage is the concept that stressors are creative opportunities and puzzles that can be solved. Patients are taught to be able to differentiate between their stressors and the reactions that come from them. In other words, they are able to tell the difference between the unchangeable and the changeable in order for their coping strategy to be adjusted accordingly. The effort of acceptance-based coping is appropriate for parts of situations that cannot be changed, while more active interventions are appropriate for more changeable stressors.

In the last phase, which is the application and following through, the therapist usually provides the patient with opportunities to practice the skills of coping that they have learned. The patients are encouraged to use a variety of simulation methods to help increase the realism of coping practice, including modeling, visualization exercise, vicarious learning, and role-playing for stressful situations. Also, simple repetition of the behavioral practice of coping routines until they are well-learned and easy to act out.

Chapter 12:

Leave Stress Behind. Live A Happier Life

"To live a happy life, very little is required; it is all contained inside yourself, in your way of thinking."

- *Marcus Aurelius*

This is your life. You will only get one chance to live it. We don't get to go back in time and redo any of this. So, you have to ask yourself in all honestly, how you want to feel in later life?

Do you want to look back and regret how much time you spent being stressed out?

Do you want to feel as though you wasted time focusing too much on the negative parts of life?

Do you want to regret losing relationships because you were unable to cope with stress?

Or do you want to look back and feel like you had the life you wanted?

Do you want to look back and feel proud of yourself for getting through your stressful moments?

When it comes to stress, we've got to get perspective on things. We need to have fun and enjoy our lives. Yes, we need to get things done and we need to make money. Those are unavoidable parts of life. But they don't mean that we have to be all work and no play. They don't mean that we can't take care of ourselves in the meantime. They don't mean that we have to miss our children growing up or that we waste our youthful vibrance trying to be more serious adults. Sure, life is serious. But it's also fun, exciting, fulfilling, and free.

For each of us, stress will come and go. We will go through tough times. We will have a hard time seeing the good parts of life when we're consumed by all the unavoidable mundanities. This does not, however, have to be the case all of the time. There are things we can do to lessen the stress we feel and get greater enjoyment and peace from our lives.

Getting structure in our lives works.

Keeping our bodies healthy works.

Taking the time to think about our feelings and experiences is beneficial.

Taking time to have fun work.

Being excited about personal growth works.

Maintaining boundaries in our relationships works.

You are full of answers to stress's most prominent problems now. All there is to do now is to be committed to giving yourself the life you desire. Go easy on yourself. Be kind to yourself. And remember, try not to take yourself too seriously. This moment should be a turning point for you. What are you going to do with it?

"The past cannot be changed. The future is still in your power"

Conclusion

It is plain to see that stress can have a major effect on your health and wellbeing. And if you're feeling stressed, the best thing you can do is to sort things out.

Determine what is causing your stress first and foremost. It may be that it stems from something internal, like an excessive workload or illness, or it might be something external - for example, financial issues or relationship problems. Once you've figured out what's causing the issue, you'll need to decide what steps to take to either eliminate the problem or change how it impacts you.

It's crucial that you don't allow stress to become a habit. The best way to stop the habit is by recognizing it. If you are serious about overcoming stress and will only be able to do so if you control the cause, you need to take action.

Here are a few thoughts on how to deal with your stress:

1. Understand the cause of your stress. Once you've identified why your stress is occurring then what can be done about it should be clear (hence the title of this article). If you don't know the reason for your stress, you'll have no choice but to fight it.

2. Adopt a new lifestyle. Make sure that you're eating well and sleeping well and get yourself exercise on a regular basis. These things are the key to putting an end to stress once and for all, as they combat stress from within rather than from without.

3. Examine your thoughts during stressful times. Achieving emotional control is important, because no matter how much effort you put into solving an emotional problem with your thoughts, it won't work if your mindset remains at its most stressed state as well. If you want to overcome stress, it's important that you identify your negative thoughts and work to change them.

4. Keep a healthy life balance. Stress can make it difficult to strike a balance between work and leisure time. In order to continue living well, maintain an active lifestyle and have time for your relationships, make sure that your strong work ethic doesn't jeopardize any of these things.

5. Recognize the signs of stress. In order to reduce stress and recognize it when it occurs, you must develop the ability to identify when you are stressed.

6. Employ a long-term strategy. Forming a long-term strategy for success is the best method to combat stress. By being persistent in this area, you will eventually be able to overcome stress completely - but that takes commitment and hard work.

7. Identify healthy coping strategies. Stress management strategies have a huge impact on an individual's health and wellbeing (see above). They can help in the battle against stress by allowing perform at their best under all circumstances.

8. Don't do things that cause stressful situations or situations where you might feel stressed. If you find yourself in a situation that you know will cause stress, then it is best to cut your losses and leave the situation. You can't change what has been done, but you can stop making the same mistakes that lead to stress - because they're bad for you.

9. Keep yourself occupied. If you have any free time, now is an excellent time to put it to good use. Once you're distracted from your stressed thoughts and are no longer feeling stressed, it's best to work on some creative project instead of spending the time staring at a screen or a computer screen.

10. Strive to achieve your desired outcome. If you want to succeed and beat stress once and for all, then you need to ensure that you're working towards an outcome where you can be happy and stress-free. The more complete your picture of the future is, the easier it will be for your stress to be removed.

11. Don't give in to stress. If you can't tolerate stress (and it is affecting your life), then you don't have to suffer it any longer. The key to breaking free of a stressful situation is to

acknowledge that you are unhappy and upset, then not giving in to the desire to remain in the situation but doing something about it instead.

12. Learn to relax. There are many ways to relax, but it takes a lot of practice for one to learn how to unwind and de-stress. The simplest way is still the best - engaging in physical activity is always beneficial.

Thank You!

Hope you've enjoyed your reading experience.

So I'd like to thank you for supporting me and reading until the very end.

It will mean a lot to me and support me in creating high-quality books, for you in the future.

Thanks once again:

Warmly yours,

Steve V. Meyer

OMG! YOUR BEST MIND EVER

Download Your Free Gift

Before you go any further, why not pick up a gift from us to you?

GROWTH PRINCIPLES

If you're willing to learn and transform yourself in all the right areas,

then success is definitely for you.

So, to find out how you can do that, let's get reading.

Scan the barcode to get it before it expires!

Feel free to continue your journey with us, where you will find new resources, tools, blogs, and advanced notice of new books at...

www.booksandsummaries.com

www.ingramcontent.com/pod-product-compliance
Lightning Source LLC
Chambersburg PA
CBHW072058110526
44590CB00018B/3222